Helping Teens Cope:

Resources for School Library Media Specialists and Other Youth Workers

Jami Biles Jones, Ph.D.

Library of Congress Cataloging-in-Publication Data

Jones, Jami Biles.
 Helping teens cope : resources for school library media specialists and other youth workers / Jami Biles Jones.
     p. cm.
Includes bibliographical references and index.
 ISBN 1-58683-121-6
 1. Teenagers--Books and reading--United States. 2. Young adult fiction--Bibliography. 3. Social problems--Fiction--Bibliography. 4. Bibliotherapy for teenagers. 5. Resilience (Personality trait) in adolescence. 6. Young adults' libraries--Activity programs--United States. I. Title.
 Z1037.A1J76 2003
 028.5'5--dc21

2003012888

Published by Linworth Publishing, Inc.
480 East Wilson Bridge Road, Suite L
Worthington, Ohio 43085

Copyright © 2003 by Linworth Publishing, Inc.

All rights reserved. Purchasing this book entitles a librarian to reproduce activity sheets for use in the library within a school or entitles a teacher to reproduce activity sheets for single classroom use within a school. Other portions of the book (up to 15 pages) may be copied for staff development purposes within a single school. Standard citation information should appear on each page. The reproduction of any part of this book for an entire school or school system or for commercial use is strictly prohibited. No part of this book may be electronically reproduced, transmitted, or recorded without written permission from the publisher.

ISBN: 1-58683-121-6

5 4 3 2 1

Table of Contents

Acknowledgements v

Introduction vii

Part I: The Foundation

Chapter One	**Bibliotherapy** 1	
Chapter Two	**Resiliency** 7	
	Resiliency Books for Middle School Readers 11	
	Resiliency Books for High School Readers 13	
Chapter Three	**Mental Health Warning Signs and Symptoms** 15	

Part II: The Issues

Chapter Four	**Maltreatment: Neglect and Abuse** 17	
	Maltreatment Books for Middle School Readers 22	
	Maltreatment Books for High School Readers 25	
Chapter Five	**Substance Abuse** 29	
	Substance Abuse Books for Middle School Readers 32	
	Substance Abuse Books for High School Readers 33	
Chapter Six	**Depression and Suicide** 37	
	Depression and Suicide Books for Middle School Readers ... 40	
	Depression and Suicide Books for High School Readers 41	
Chapter Seven	**Eating Disorders and Body Image** 45	
	Eating Disorders and Body Image Books for Middle School Readers 48	
	Eating Disorders and Body Image Books for High School Readers 49	
Chapter Eight	**Self-Inflicted Violence** 51	
	Self-Inflicted Violence Books for Middle School Readers .. 54	
	Self-Inflicted Violence Books for High School Readers 55	
Chapter Nine	**Divorce** 57	
	Divorce Books for Middle School Readers 60	
	Divorce Books for High School Readers 62	

Chapter Ten	**Teen Pregnancy**	65
	Teen Pregnancy Books for Middle School Readers	67
	Teen Pregnancy Books for High School Readers	68
Chapter Eleven	**Relationship Violence**	73
	Relationship Violence Books for Middle School Readers	76
	Relationship Violence Books for High School Readers	76
Chapter Twelve	**Driving**	79
	Driving Books for Middle School Readers	81
	Driving Books for High School Readers	81
Chapter Thirteen	**Bullying and Cliques**	85
	Bullying and Cliques Books for Middle School Readers	88
	Bullying and Cliques Books for High School Readers	90

Part III: Bringing Attention to the Issues

Chapter Fourteen	Calendar of Events	93
Chapter Fifteen	Interactive Booktalking	101
Chapter Sixteen	Useful Web Sites for Youth Workers	107

References 112

Appendix A: "Must Reads" for Youth Workers 122

Appendix B: Interactive Booktalking of *Driver's Ed* by Caroline B. Cooney 124

Index 128

About the Author 134

Acknowledgements

Helping Teens Cope: Resources for School Library Media Specialists and Other Youth Workers is dedicated to Amanda. It is written to celebrate her life and the lives of other teens I have known. I owe a great debt of gratitude to Amanda's family for sharing her story with me. Her life and death have prodded me to advocate for teens and communities, schools, and libraries that promote resiliency. Now more than ever, it takes a village to raise a child.

I am forever indebted to Gail MacKenzie, my colleague at Barron Collier High School in Naples, Florida. She spent hours listening to me as I conceived the idea for this book. Whenever I doubted my ability to write this book, Gail was there to urge me on. I thank Gail for her willingness to edit the manuscript prior to its submission to Linworth Publishing. More than anyone else, Gail understands my depth of commitment to teens.

I thank Donna Miller for skillfully guiding this manuscript from its inception to the finished product. I appreciate Donna for having the foresight to realize that this book needed to be written.

I am grateful to my friend and fellow educator, Theresa Demery, for her support and encouragement over the years. I am a better librarian as a result of her friendship.

Finally, I want to thank my family. My son, Josh, has helped me to understand how teens think and feel. My husband, John, remains my most steadfast champion. He has stood by my side and patiently urged me on as I researched and wrote this book. His continued support and insights have allowed me to mature professionally.

In Memory of Amanda
1979–2001

Introduction

A 1989 report by the Carnegie Council on Adolescent Development warned that "by age 15, substantial numbers of American youth are at risk of reaching adulthood unable to adequately meet the requirements of the workplace, the commitments of relationships in families and with friends, and the responsibility of participation in a democratic society" (Hersch 12). Furthermore, the report stated that "half of all adolescents are at some risk for serious problems such as substance abuse; early, unprotected intercourse; dangerous accident-prone lifestyles; delinquent behavior; and dropping out of school" (12). In 1995, another Carnegie Foundation report stated that "adolescents are facing demands and expectations, as well as risks and threats, that are both more numerous and more serious than they were only a generation ago" (12). Little has changed since these Carnegie reports were published.

Adolescence is a time of great change. It is a metamorphosis from childhood to adulthood. For most teens, this stage of development is smooth. Some teens, though, for a variety of reasons, encounter problems during these years. The reasons will become evident after reading *Helping Teens Cope: Resources for School Library Media Specialists and Other Youth Workers*. The purpose of this book is to help public librarians, media specialists, and others who work with adolescents understand the cultural and societal influences and challenges facing teens.

The book is unique in its premise that librarians and media specialists can make a difference in the lives of teens by developing services and programs that promote resiliency. Library professionals and youth workers promote healthy teen development by encouraging reading, developing programs, and making connections. The book thoroughly summarizes the research and professional articles on many topics of adolescence including bibliotherapy, resiliency theory, and issues impacting teens. The author read, studied, and synthesized numerous books, journal articles, dissertations, and Internet resources. The recommendations for working with teens and building teen book collections are grounded in research conducted by social scientists, educators, and librarians. Professionals who are interested in reading other books to help youth deal with their challenges may want to read a 1997 title by Beth and Carol Doll, *Bibliotherapy with Young People: Librarians and Mental Health Professionals Working Together*. Other titles of interest are included in the Greenwood Press series *Using Literature to Help Troubled Teenagers*. The scarcity of books produced by the library profession on the topic of troubled teens reflects the overall dearth of books published on this topic in general. For the concerned parent and librarian, many books have been written about children and their development. However, there are fewer resources about adolescents. As a society, we have mostly turned our backs on teens.

Readers will benefit from this book in four important ways. First, by understanding the issues, challenges, and problems facing teens, library professionals and other youth workers are more likely to develop libraries and organizations that are teen-centered. This is vitally important because "the young people of today represent 100% of the human capital on which the future health and success of America rests" (Lerner and Lerner xxxix). We cannot develop teen-friendly programs and services without input from teens. This input, as well as our understanding of adolescents and the societal challenges facing them, will lead to the development of organizations that make a difference in the lives of young people.

Second, the book is a tool to build collections that are meaningful and supportive of teens. One finding from the Kauai Longitudinal Study (Werner and Smith 205) on resiliency shows that reading promotes self-esteem and is a protective factor for at-risk children and teens. Reading can help teens make sense of the biological, psychological, and cultural challenges they are facing. Therefore, by providing teens with books to help them learn about and successfully cope with their challenges, librarians have a far greater impact on teens than they think. After reading this title, library professionals and other youth workers will understand the importance of their services in the development of emotionally and physically healthy teens.

Third, the book will take the guesswork out of programming because library professionals and youth workers will more clearly understand teens and their needs. By applying the results of resiliency research to program development, librarians will be more likely to develop effective programs. Research indicates the types of programs that benefit teens focus on reading, making connections and mentoring, supporting teens' interests in hobbies and personal development, and building skills in information and problem solving.

Fourth, this book will enable readers to become leaders and advocates in their communities because they will learn what makes a difference in the lives of teens. They will understand that libraries may need to collaborate with other community organizations to establish policies and services that support all of its youth.

This book is arranged in three sections: The Foundation; The Issues; and Bringing Attention to the Issues. The first section, The Foundation, includes three chapters: Bibliotherapy, Resiliency, and Mental Health Warning Signs and Symptoms. This section is the underpinning for the book. It is hoped that readers who did not previously understand the importance of books and bibliotherapy in helping teens cope will gain this understanding. Readers will also learn about the protective factors of resiliency. Resiliency is the ability to succeed even in the face adversity. This fascinating body of research conducted by social scientists has great influence on libraries because it proves that what we do makes a difference. For instance, when the emphasis is on reading and teaching problem-solving, social, and information skills, then librarians and other youth workers are building resiliency in teens. Because some challenges teens face are potentially life-threatening, the chapter on Mental Health Warning Signs and Symptoms will help readers determine the point at which other authority figures need to be called in and informed about the teen's situation.

The second section, The Issues, consists of the identification of 10 problems and challenges that may be experienced by teens. The 10 issues are: maltreatment, substance abuse, depression and suicide, eating disorders and body image, self-inflicted violence, divorce, teen pregnancy, relationship violence, driving, and bullying and cliques. Each issue is defined and the symptoms and consequences are identified. The description of the issue is followed by reviews of young adult fiction books in which the characters are dealing with these issues. For some of the issues, one that comes to mind is self-inflicted violence, there is a need for more fiction books on this topic Few self-inflicted violence books are written for the middle school audience. This is unfortunate because many times these issues begin to crop up and are noticed shortly after the difficult transition from elementary to middle or junior high school. Another issue, date rape, has few books written for the early adolescent. This may be because during this early period of adolescence, teens are generally more interested in group activities containing both genders and are only beginning to pair off. For the most part, coupling is an activity of high school teens.

It is helpful for teens to understand that their peers struggle with similar issues. Part of the teenage experience is the feeling that they are the only ones facing a particular problem, even though, in reality, many of their peers in middle and high schools across America are in the same predicament. The official term for this intense self-focus is "adolescent egocentrism." It is the heightened self-consciousness that emerges out of the interaction between the physical, cognitive, and social changes teens are undergoing (Camarena 633). Reading about other teens can ease "adolescent egocentrism" and isolation.

Most of the young adult books reviewed in the second section have copyright dates later than 1995. However, a few timeless "classics" with earlier copyright dates are also included. This decision was made for two reasons. First, books written before 1995 may be unavailable because they are out of print. Second, even if available, an older book may be dated in its language and sense of the issue. Teens are hyper-sensitive to outdated slang terms and life situations in which they cannot relate.

The books are categorized for either middle school or high school students. Books for middle schoolers tend to have middle school-aged characters. The treatment of the issue is milder. The issue may be specific to this age group. For instance, bullying is regarded as a serious middle school problem. Likewise, books categorized for high school students portray high school-aged characters. These books may be more graphic. There may be stronger language. In deciding whether or not to purchase these books, the author suggests that they be previewed by the librarian or youth worker. Some of these books may have more "issue" and language than may be appropriate or suitable for a particular collection.

The third section, Bringing Attention to the Issues, consists of an extensive calendar of events and ideas for programs. In addition, a chapter on interactive booktalking provides the foundation for a new type of booktalking that more fully meets the needs of teens by providing opportunities for dialogue and discussion. Interactive booktalking is one way that library professionals and youth workers can bring attention to and counteract the negative effects of issues such as substance abuse, anorexia, bullying, and self-harm.

The book includes two appendixes. Appendix A is an annotated listing of books youth workers will want to consider purchasing for their professional collections. Appendix B is an interactive booktalk of *Driver's Ed* by Caroline B. Cooney. An index is provided to make topics and titles more accessible to the reader.

"America's own adolescents have become strangers. They are a tribe apart, remote, mysterious, vaguely threatening" (Hersch 14). This book is a tool to motivate library professionals and youth workers to work on behalf of teens so they no longer remain "a tribe apart."

Part I: The Foundation

Chapter One

Bibliotherapy

Throughout history, even as far back as the early Egyptians and Plato, books have been recognized for their healing power and ability to lift the human spirit. However, as the practice and technique of using books to help solve problems became more established, tension and conflict erupted between the role of the librarian and other professionals in bibliotherapy. The first time that the term "bibliotherapy" was officially used was in August 1916 in an article in *Atlantic Magazine* by Samuel Crothers in which he described a technique of prescribing books to hospital patients who need help understanding their problems (Crothers qtd. in Myracle 36). By the early 1920s, bibliotherapy techniques developed by Sadie Peterson Delaney, chief librarian of the U.S. Veterans Administration Hospital in Tuskegee, Alabama, were utilized to treat the psychological, emotional, and physical needs of African-American war veterans. Between 1924 and 1958, Delaney received worldwide recognition for the bibliotherapy techniques that she had so finely tuned and promoted. She spoke at major conferences and held lectures in conjunction with psychology courses, and she was actively training other librarians in the practice of bibliotherapy. In addition to books, Delaney used "plants, flowers, wall maps, and posters for their psychological effects" (Gubert 125). She developed programs, literary clubs, story hours, and clubs to reduce internal pressures and alleviate the boredom and loneliness of hospitalized patients (127).

In November 1937, William Menninger, founder of the Menninger Clinic, wrote that since bibliotherapy was a treatment method, it must be directed by the physician. Menninger minimized Delaney's efforts in bibliotherapy and limited the role of the librarian to purchasing and distributing books only after they had been selected and prescribed by the physician (Wolpow and Askov 2001 606).

In her 1949 doctoral dissertation, Caroline Shrodes linked bibliotherapy to the three independent states of psychotherapy called identification, catharsis, and insight. Shrodes suggested that "bibliotherapy was effective because it allows the reader to identify with a character and realize that others have these problems, too. As the character works through the problem, the reader becomes emotionally involved in the struggle and ultimately achieves insight about his or her own situation" (Myracle 36). Today, identification, catharsis, and insight remain central to the bibliotherapy experience. In addition, children and teens benefit from the role-playing, problem-solving, and goal-setting aspects of bibliotherapy (Doll and Doll 14).

Since these early definitions and practices of bibliotherapy, the controversy has continued. There are two possible explanations for this continued controversy. First, the lack of longitudinal studies raises questions about the long-term efficacy of bibliotherapy since most of the empirical research studies of bibliotherapy have been conducted for fewer than 14 weeks. Second, in the vast majority of research, whether empirical or case studies, the interaction with teacher, therapist, or group has proven to be more important than the actual reading (Wolpow and Askov 1998 51).

Is bibliotherapy simply, as suggested by Bernstein, "helping with books" (159) or is it part of a treatment plan to be conducted by credentialed mental health professionals? The literature indicates that "bibliotherapy moves along the continuum from simple reading guidance to comprehensive therapy programs" and "at its simplest, it is the private and personal insight that a child gains from a book. On the other end of the continuum, bibliotherapy is a more serious and complex form of therapy that occurs between the seriously disturbed client and the highly trained mental health professional" (Doll and Doll 7).

Because definitions of bibliotherapy vary, some practitioners and researchers have addressed the definitional confusion by specifying types of bibliotherapy. Gladding and Gladding call a minimalist version of bibliotherapy "reactive bibliotherapy" in which children are assigned books to read and react to them (12). A second form of bibliotherapy, "interactive bibliotherapy," is the process of growth, change, and healing that occurs as a result of guided and facilitated dialogue about the material (Doll and Doll 7). Another attempt to categorize bibliotherapy is the distinction that Lack makes between "developmental bibliotherapy" which is the personalization of literature to help "children cope with developmental needs, typical problems that do not need advanced therapeutic intervention" and "clinical bibliotherapy" which focuses on specific psychological and emotional problems (29).

Whichever definition is embraced, Doll and Doll identify seven major purposes for bibliotherapy:

- To foster personal insight and self-understanding among children and youth who read;
- To help children and teens experience catharsis, or the release of emotional or psychological tension that occurs when readers experience the feelings of the characters they are reading about;
- To use literature as a catalyst to solve day-to-day problems and cope with developmental change;
- To help children and teens change the ways in which they interact with or behave toward others;
- To promote effective and satisfying relationships with other people;
- To be a source of information for youth when they face specific problems, such as divorce, blended families, and sickness, that may set them apart from their peers; and
- To alleviate boredom and promote self-growth (7).

Two types of professional reading that can help librarians and youth workers learn about the beneficial techniques and practices of bibliotherapy are anecdotal accounts and experimental research studies. Recent anecdotal accounts indicate that bibliotherapy is being used regularly and consistently to help students deal with emotional, academic, and behavioral problems. Wolpow and Askov describe practices used by literacy teachers that "show students how to glean a personal understanding from what they read and write" (1998, 51). These practices also illustrate the importance of a literacy teacher to a bibliotherapy treatment team. Amer writes about pediatric nurses using books with children who have diabetes and short stature disease to help enhance their understanding, self-esteem, and adjustment to their illnesses (94). In another anecdotal article, a student fulfilling her teaching internship in an alternative school for high school students used sports literature as a catalyst to contemplate "issues and behaviors whose scope extends far beyond the playing field or locker room" (Carter 309). Because of erratic student attendance patterns, Carter found that "minibibliotherapy" sessions in which the text could be read and discussed in single periods worked best. Sridhar and Vaughn write about a teacher who used books in a bibliotherapeutic method to help special education students recognize and learn to cope with their various behavioral problems. The sessions consisted of four steps: to determine the problems to be addressed; to introduce students to the theme of the book, to encourage them to compare their experiences with the situations in the book, and to make predictions about the book and its characters; to ask directed questions during the reading; and after the reading, to initiate a discussion to help students process the story and determine alternate behaviors for the characters (76). Manning and Manning describe ways that books can be used to help children of alcoholics acknowledge the problems they are facing at home and learn appropriate coping strategies and mechanisms (720).

Lendowsky and Lendowsky note that bibliotherapy is consistent with the goals of education, reading, and the theory that a positive self-concept is essential to learning. Bibliotherapy may be especially beneficial with learning disabled adolescents who are prone to feelings of inferiority and failure. Teachers infused bibliotherapy and personal guidance into already established reading strategies because "reading such stories reinforced their feelings of 'normalcy' and helped students realize that they were not alone in facing adolescence's problems and the special problems created by their disabilities" (181). Because many learning disabled students have limited reading abilities, the teacher often accomplishes bibliotherapy by reading out loud to the students and by using books on audiotapes. Kramer conjectures that bibliotherapy may be one of the ways to help promote attitudes of respect and acceptance in inclusion classrooms in which students with special needs are mixed in with regular education students (36).

An experimental study in Israel was designed to test the effectiveness of bibliotherapy in reducing aggressive behavior among children and adolescents. The research showed that the treatment group benefited by bibliotherapy and increased self-control, self-awareness, and enhanced social skills. The experimental group that received the bibliotherapy intervention "appreciated the opportunity to release disturbing feelings" (Shechtman 165).

In each of the practices identified above, educators and social scientists note that it is critical that the adult facilitating the bibliotherapy be thoroughly familiar with the books being used and only utilize appropriate and realistic books that provide a hopeful conclusion. According to Pardeck, books can be used with teens to help them cope with problems such as family breakdown, foster care, and adoption. The four stages of bibliotherapy used by Pardeck are:

- To identify the problems or issues encountered by the teen;
- To read and select books that can help teens with their problems, address their interests, and are written at the appropriate reading level;
- To introduce the book while keeping in mind that books should be suggested rather than prescribed; and
- To utilize follow-up activities because research indicates that to be effective, the reading of a book must be accompanied by discussion and counseling (423).

Follow-up bibliotherapy activities can include creative writing, art activities, discussion, and role- playing (Pardeck 423). Students may utilize their creative writing skills to develop a synopsis of the book by changing the point of view from the one who told the story to another character, to make a daily schedule for the character with which the adolescent can most identify and compare it to his or her own schedule, to compose a diary for a character in the book, and to write a letter from one character in the book to another, or from the adolescent to one of the characters.

Art activities that support spatial intelligence include the creation of:

- Maps that illustrate story events, with the adolescent using his or her imagination to provide details not given in the book;
- Collages consisting of pictures pasted on a piece of cardboard to illustrate the events in the story;
- Pictures drawn in a sequence of important incidents in the book; and
- Mobiles that represent key events or characters using the adolescent's own drawings or pictures cut from magazines.

Discussion and role-playing can include round-table discussions concerning a decision one of the characters must make, discussions about the strong and weak points of a character with whom the adolescent identifies, role-playing an incident in the book, recreating the book in another format such as a play or music, and holding a mock trial concerning an incident in the book, with students playing the parts of defendant, lawyers, judge, jury, and witnesses.

The above activities support the following intelligences as defined by Howard Gardner (*The Seven Types of Intelligences*):

- Interpersonal—being aware of other's feelings and intentions;
- Bodily-kinesthetic—the use of mental and physical abilities to role-play a scene from the book;
- Spatial—the ability to recreate the book into another format; and
- Musical—composing music or writing lyrics to explain the book.

Many of these follow-up activities can be augmented with technology. For instance, students could create letters, a synopsis of the story, or diaries using a word processing program or a weblog, which is an easy-to-update personal diary on the Internet. PowerPoint™ or HyperStudio™ could be used to develop a collage of pictures copied from the Internet, scanned from photos, or taken with a digital camera. Literature webs or sequences could be developed using a mind mapping software program, such as Inspiration™, that can be downloaded for a free 30-day trial from <http://www.Inspiration.com>. In addition to the affective and problem-solving benefits of bibliotherapy, technology can heighten interest in the project, especially among special needs students. Learning new skills or developing existing technology skills increases self-esteem and confidence, improves reading, and provides a forum in which to share their projects with other teens and a caring teacher, librarian, or youth worker.

Librarians and media specialists can utilize bibliotherapy to bring attention to the issues described in this book, enhance literacy, and teach problem-solving skills. In this way, books can be used to help teens develop strategies to overcome their challenges. Interactive Booktalking, which is described in Part III of this book, is one method that can be used in a class setting to make connections, support reading, and encourage problem solving.

Chapter Two

Resiliency

It is estimated that between one-half and two-thirds of poverty stricken children growing up in families with mentally ill, alcoholic, abusive, or criminally involved parents are able to overcome hardships and go on to live meaningful and productive lives (Edwards 15). Mental health experts and educators have long wondered why some children and teens are able to withstand great problems, while others are not. This ability to "bounce back successfully despite exposure to severe risks" is called resiliency (Benard 44). Children are able to adjust to these potentially damaging conditions by developing and drawing on their resiliency (Edwards 15). Researchers have found that resilient children have both internal and external assets that protect them from the long-lasting detrimental harm which may result from adversity and serious problems.

> "It's like the hidden secret that no one tells you. We can all be beautiful girls, Colie. It's so easy. It's like Dorothy clicking her heels to go home. You could do it all along."—*Keeping the Moon* by Sarah Dessen

The four internal assets or characteristics that are found in resilient children are: social competence or the ability to establish positive relationships with adults and peers, effective problem-solving skills, autonomy and a sense of purpose, and the ability to plan for the future. Resilient adolescents have good self-esteem, a positive view of themselves, and possess educational and occupational aspirations (Howard, Dryden, and Johnson 311). Griffin et al. likens internal assets to "competence skills," which are "learned attitudes and aptitudes, manifested as capacities for confronting, actively struggling with, and mastering life problems through the use of cognitive and social skills" (194). Promoting competence skills and internal assets is a way for children and adolescents to successfully meet developmental challenges and to avoid at-risk situations such as substance abuse and unwanted pregnancies.

In addition to internal factors that protect children and teens from adversity and problems, external factors in the family, school, and community also protect and help build resiliency. These external factors are: strong relationships with caring adults, meaningful opportunities to participate in the family, school, or community, high expectations to succeed and contribute to society, and activities that allow teens to build decision-making skills (Howard, Dryden, and Johnson 312).

The Kauai Longitudinal Study, one of the most important pieces of social science research about this topic, answers the question, "What factors promote resiliency in children?" All the children born in 1955 on the Hawaiian Island of Kauai became part of this study "to assess the long-term consequences of prenatal complications and adverse rearing conditions on the individual's development and adaptation to life" (Krovetz 8). The children were followed shortly before birth until they were 31 or 32 years of age. The authors of the study, Emmy E. Werner and Ruth S. Smith, identified many adverse conditions, such as poverty, prolonged absence of mother and father because of separation and divorce, and school failure, that put children at risk. However, they also identified many factors that protect children and teens from the effects of these adverse conditions (157).

In this well-designed research study, Werner and Smith found that resilient children had good temperaments and were easy to get along with. They had supportive caregivers, good physical health, and self-esteem. They also had an internal locus of control, meaning that they feel they are in control of their lives. Werner and Smith found that positive relationships were key to protecting children from various adversities, and that most children have self-righting tendencies and can flourish even under the most difficult circumstances (Howard, Dryden, and Johnson 313). Although many children are able to overcome two, three, or even four challenges, when the lives of families exposed to seven or eight risks were studied, not one resilient child was found (Katz 205).

Specifically, Werner and Smith found that 43% of the study's most resilient adults had at least some college education and were competent readers. One of the most potent predictors of successful adult adaptation is competence in reading by fourth grade (Werner and Smith 176). In addition, the resilient adults in this study remember one or two teachers who made a difference in their lives. Nowhere were the differences between resilient individuals and their peers more apparent than in the goals they set for themselves: career and job success was the highest priority on the agenda of the resilient men and women but was the lowest priority for the least resilient individuals and those who had difficulties in adolescence (Krovetz 9). Werner and Smith's research has been confirmed in a more recent study by Zimmerman, Bingenheimer, and Notaro in which the protective factor of a caring adult or a mentor was vital to the development of resiliency. Their research indicated that teens with mentors were less likely to smoke marijuana or be involved in nonviolent delinquency, had more positive attitudes toward school, and reported lower levels of problem behavior. Having a mentor partially offset the effect of negative peer influences (221).

In the past, educators adhered to the reactive problem focus model in which educational policies, programs, and interventions were developed and delivered to students after they had been identified for being at risk. According to the 1989 Carnegie Council on Adolescent Development report, half of all America's adolescents are "at some risk for serious problems like substance abuse; early, unprotected sexual intercourse; dangerous accident-prone lifestyles; delinquent behavior; and dropping out of school" (Hersch 12). Because many teens can be labeled at-risk at one time or another, experts now believe that it is almost impossible—and the funding is not available—to develop programs that specifically address each of these risky behaviors. There is now a shift away from identifying risks and developing specific programs to assuage those risks to creating supportive and challenging environments for teens. Resiliency Theory is a proactive model that is based on building resiliency by helping teens acquire capabilities, skills, and assets to overcome present and future difficulties and challenges. Resiliency Theory, which emphasizes strengthening the environment, not fixing the kids, is the belief that every person can overcome adversity if important and protective factors are present (Krovetz 6).

It takes a concerted effort by families, communities, and schools to raise emotionally healthy and resilient teens in this New Millennium. Families can foster resiliency by providing consistent care and support during infancy, childhood, and adolescence. This involves effective parenting (Masten 232), providing adequate and consistent parental role models, spending time with teens, and providing firm and consistent guidance without repressive or rejecting attitudes (Howard, Dryden, and Johnson 312).

Communities can foster resiliency by providing strong social service agencies that can offset such adversities as poverty and parental neglect. Communities can also build resiliency by providing teens with leadership opportunities to participate on boards and committees, and internships that bring them into contact with adults who can be role models and guides. The Carnegie Council on Adolescent Development report warned that "by age 15, substantial numbers of American youth are at risk of reaching adulthood unable to adequately meet the requirements of the workplace, the commitments of relationships in families and with friends, and the responsibilities of participation in democratic society" (Hersch 12).

Schools can foster resiliency by providing teens with achievement-oriented and positive experiences in sports, music, or clubs; by creating opportunities to assume responsible leadership positions in school government; by encouraging connections with caring teachers; and by offering opportunities to develop social success. Schools with good academic programs and attentive, caring teachers build resiliency. School success and competence are best supported through a practical and relevant curriculum and attentive school personnel (Howard, Dryden, and Johnson 312).

Librarians and media specialists can foster resiliency too. They are in a unique position to promote resiliency among teens by focusing their efforts in the following five areas.

First, connect with teens. Werner and Smith found that "during adolescence, a caring teacher was an important protective factor for boys and girls who succeeded against the odds" (178). To the adolescent, this caring adult became a strong role model, a confidant, and was important in his or her life. Teens who have friendships with adults outside their families feel supported, are more social, and less depressed (Hair, Jager, and Garrett 2). Media specialists can become important in the lives of teens who are lonely, new to the school, or perhaps do not feel they belong. Teens need a special place where they can feel safe from social pressures and can hang with their friends, be with other like-minded students, or just be by themselves. Libraries and media centers are safe places where students can learn about ideas and connect with caring adults who can protect and insulate them from the negative effects of stress, challenges, and loneliness. Media specialists are in a unique position to connect with teens because they often work with them to find books and resources on a one-to-one basis.

According to Patricia Hersch, author of *A Tribe Apart: A Journey into the Heart of American Adolescence*, today's teens have little involvement with adults. She writes that teens "spend virtually all of their discretionary time without companionship or supervision by responsible adults" (21). At a time when teens need adults to emulate, those around them may be working too many hours, divorcing, remarrying, and living lives that are very separate. This uncommitted and unsupervised time "gives this generation unequaled freedom of determination in many areas of their lives" (Hersch 21). This time could be used productively to gain new resiliency-building skills and resources. But too often it is wasted time that sanctions risky behaviors such as substance abuse, unplanned and unprotected sex, and delinquency. After-school programs and neighborhood organizations can serve as important resources by shielding teens, especially those who are growing up in inner cities, from some of the risks that surround them.

Second, develop collections of interest to teens that are both developmentally appropriate and stimulating. Werner and Smith found that reading was "one of the most potent predictors of successful adaptation among high risk children" (205). The role of the librarian and media specialist to encourage reading is unique because it extends beyond the school's curriculum to promote interests, skills, and character development. Through reading, teens develop strategies for successful living and problem solving. They develop recreational and lifelong reading habits to help withstand life's difficulties. Reading is especially beneficial to teens because it helps them realize that others—both fictional characters and real people—are dealing with similar issues and challenges. Reading may become a solace during stressful times.

Teen reading, and resiliency, is supported when teens have access to books and materials that interest them. Strong collections are imperative because "research supports the common sense view that when books are readily available, when the print environment is rich, more reading is done" (Krashen 33). According to Werner and Smith's findings, librarians and media specialists promote resiliency when they develop programs such as book clubs, booktalking events, lectures, and displays that stimulate reading. Reading can be promoted by organizing a cadre of teens to write book reviews that are uploaded to the library's Web site or published in the local or school newspaper. In addition, a local author or an instructor can work with teens to write poetry and short stories for the library's literary magazine. This may be a cathartic experience for the teens.

Third, teach teens how to deal effectively with their everyday problems by asking the right questions and utilizing proper search strategies to identify options and solutions. Two problem-solving skills are especially important. The first is "planning which facilitates seeing oneself in control" (Benard 44). The second is "resourcefulness in seeking help from others" (44). The steps of problem solving are to:

- Identify and define the problem;
- List possible options and solutions;
- Evaluate all options and solutions;
- Choose one option or solution;
- Make a plan and carry it out; and
- Evaluate the problem and solution (Welker).

By using problem-solving and information search techniques, teens will become autonomous and responsible adults (Welker). In addition, because adolescence is a stressful period, teens benefit by being taught coping skills to control or reduce their pressures (Feldman 427). Specifically, librarians and media specialists can arrange for workshops and lectures to help teens understand and prepare for the challenges of adolescence. Programs and workshops that teach organizational and planning skills, resume writing skills, stress management, skills in searching for information, and job hunting strategies are helpful. Other programs can teach teens about the importance of healthy eating, hygiene, exercise, hair care, cosmetics, and organizing and caring for their wardrobe.

Fourth, teach social skills. These skills enable teens to develop and maintain high-quality relationships that are integral to friendships, romance, academics, and business. Teens with well-developed social skills are psychologically healthier, have improved academic performances, and more successful relationships (Hair, Jager, and Garrett 1). One way librarians and media specialists support and enhance social skills is by involving teens in the development and implementation of programs. For instance, public librarians might consider initiating a teen board of middle and high school representatives who act as conduits to pass information back and forth between the school and public library. The public library can use this information to develop a newsletter or television program consisting of book and movie reviews, poetry, fashion and beauty tips, sports news, and other items of interest to teens. Some of these news items can be developed in journalism or English class and reformatted for inclusion in the newsletter or television program.

Fifth, provide opportunities to learn about hobbies and develop new interests (Krovetz 9). Hobbies and interests help teens look toward the future, develop competence, and feel good about themselves. Teens can be encouraged to learn new hobbies through lectures, demonstrations, and workshops. The library or media center can sponsor a hobby day or "Hobby Fest" to bring experts and enthusiasts together with interested teens.

Librarians and media specialists must consider five points when developing teen-centered programs that build resiliency. First, it is important that the adults who are involved with teens like and enjoy them. Adults need to be trained to work with teens and to understand the vagaries of this developmental period. Second, it is vital that teens be involved in the planning and implementation of programs. Without teen input, librarians and media specialists cannot be assured they are developing programs that teens want and need. Third, the number of teens attending a program is not the sole measurement of its success. Because many teens lack parental support and are lost in the "bigness" of schools, smaller programs provide the intimacy and warm environment they relish. Fourth, middle and high school students should not be automatically grouped together in the same programs because the needs of the two age groups are different. High school-aged students may be reluctant to attend programs with middle schoolers. Even though both age groups may serve together on the library's board, whenever possible, programs should be designed for either middle or high school-aged students to meet their developmental needs. Fifth, rules should be kept to a minimum and decided by teens and adults together. In this way, teens learn how to compromise and work in a committee environment. Teens benefit emotionally when their opinions are valued and respected.

Resiliency Books for Middle School Readers

Couloumbis, Audrey. *Say Yes*. **New York: G.P. Putnam's Sons. 2002.**
From the book's opening words, "Wednesday morning is like any other but different," readers know that something significant is about to happen to Casey, a 12-year-old New York City girl. Casey's father is dead and she lives with her stepmother, Sylvia, a dreamer who desperately wants to remarry. Although

Sylvia is the adult, it is Casey whose feet are firmly planted on the ground. Casey is vocal about not liking the men Sylvia brings home and isn't too eager to have her father replaced. Because Sylvia hopes that Casey will eventually accept this newest fiancé, she decides to run away with him even though this leaves Casey all alone. Casey's attempts to hide the situation from her friends and neighbors should win her an Academy Award. Many teens who have been emotionally deserted by their mother or father in favor of a new love interest will relate to this story.

Draper, Sharon M. *Double Dutch*. New York: Atheneum Books for Young Readers. 2002.
Draper has crafted a memorable story about strong, middle-class, African-American teens who overcome severe obstacles with help from their friends. Delia's problem is that she is in eighth grade and still cannot read, Randy's father disappeared and he has not been seen or heard from in six weeks, and everybody in school is scared to death of the Tolliver twins after they admit their antisocial inclinations on a national television talk show. Sometimes teens adopt a fearsome exterior to bolster low self-esteem. The book's action takes place in the two weeks leading up to Delia and her friends' competition in the state and national Double Dutch tournament. This book shows how each character uses the protective factors of resiliency—connections, reading, sports, and problem solving—to meet his or her challenges head-on.

Karr, Kathleen. *The Great Turkey Walk*. New York: Farrar, Straus and Giroux. 1998.
After repeating third grade for the fourth time, Simon Green's teacher, Miss Rogers, tells him that he's learned about all that she can teach him, and it is time for him to spread his wings and move on. With encouragement and a small loan, Simon's business acumen flourishes as he challenges himself by walking 1,000 turkeys from eastern Missouri to Denver. Along the way, Simon finds three others in need of their own break in life to join the turkey-walking expedition. Simon's business venture is a great success. With the money Simon and his partners earn, they repay Miss Rogers and start a lucrative farm outside Denver. *The Great Turkey Walk* is a delightful book that sends a strong message that everyone has talents just waiting to be discovered.

Paulsen, Gary. *My Life in Dog Years*. New York: Delacorte Press. 1998.
My Life in Dog Years is Gary Paulsen's autobiography that unfolds in the stories about his dogs. In this book, Paulsen shares with young teens his lonely childhood in which he was dragged from military base to military base by his alcoholic parents. Paulsen's way of dealing with loneliness and neglectful parents was to camp and hunt with his trusty and devoted dogs. The stories about his dogs range from humorous to tragic; but it is clear that each and every one of them has helped Paulsen cope and develop resiliency. After reading this book, teens will have a better understanding of the nature themes in Paulsen's books, as well as how to make lemonade from lemons.

Resiliency Books for High School Readers

Bauer, Joan. *Backwater*. New York: Puffin Books. 1999.
If Ivy had not inherited the distinctive Breedlove chin, she would surely have felt compelled to sue the hospital for switching her at birth. The non-aggressive Ivy has lived her life surrounded by fabulously successful family members who have relentlessly communicated to her their expectations that she follow in their footsteps. Ivy, however, is more like her deceased mother and is drawn to people, history, and genealogy — not law. While researching her family tree, Ivy learns about Great-Aunt Josephine, the black sheep of the family, who preferred to live by herself in the mountains rather than conform to the expectations of the overpowering Breedlove clan. Ivy is so intrigued by what she learns that she defies her family and hires a guide to lead her high up in the mountains to Josephine's complex. After experiencing cold, isolation, a near death experience, and love — in that order — Ivy learns that she cannot pretend to be something she is not.

Dessen, Sarah. *Keeping the Moon*. New York: Viking. 1999.
Colie Sparks is used to being labeled the new fat girl in town. Even after dieting and sweating off a gazillion pounds, the catty and mean girls at school will not let her forget that she is a big loser and will always be fat in their eyes. In this story, Colie spends the summer with her unusual and colorful aunt while her mother, a fitness guru with her own infomercials, is off in Europe promoting her fitness plan. After Colie finds special girlfriends who pep talk her into reclaiming her self-esteem, she gradually morphs from a teen with bad hair, baggy clothes, and a lip ring into a shining star. There is a powerful scene in which Colie, who has a history of being friendless and bullied, finally stands up for herself. Dessen has produced the ultimate "chick book."

Flaming, Allen, and Kate Scowen. *My Crazy Life: How I Survived My Family*. Toronto: Annick Press. 2002.
The collective wisdom from teens who have lived through trying family circumstances, such as poverty, mental illness, divorce, death, and abuse, is contained in this slim volume that teens will devour. Each of the 10 stories is followed by the teens' advice for enduring similarly chaotic situations. Their advice parallels resiliency research: develop relationships with caring adults, use problem-solving skills to minimize the situation, become involved in sports and activities, and stay focused and true to yourself.

Spinelli, Jerry. *Stargirl*. New York: A. Knopf. 2000.
The teens at Mica Area High School in Arizona have never encountered anybody quite like Stargirl: she dresses too funky, plays the ukulele in the cafeteria, sends congratulatory messages and gifts to people she does not know, says hello to everyone — not just the popular kids — and has a pet rat named Cinnamon. At first the students love her differences, but when Stargirl refuses to conform to the unspoken rules, they turn on her and try to break her spirit. Even though Stargirl is shunned by students, she leaves a lasting legacy at Mica Area High

School. It has the only marching band in the state—most likely in the world—with a ukulele, and the school has a club called the Sunflowers whose members promise to do "one nice thing per day for someone other than myself." This is a clever and powerful book about the importance of staying true to one's own personality and style.

Chapter Three

Mental Health Warning Signs and Symptoms

Many teens are affected by mental health problems. According to the Substance Abuse and Mental Health Services Administration (SAMHSA), at any given time, one in five children and adolescents is suffering from mental health problems. At least one in 10—or as many as six million teens—may have a serious emotional disturbance. Most of these teens will not receive mental health treatment or counseling because their problems are not recognized for what they are. The causes of teen mental health problems are complicated and can be caused by biology, environment, or both. Biological causes can be genetics, chemical imbalances in the body, and damage to the central nervous system. Environmental factors that can put teens at risk of developing mental health problems are: exposure to toxins, such as high levels of lead; witnessing or experiencing violence and maltreatment; stress related to poverty, discrimination, or other hardships; and loss of important people through death, divorce, or broken relationships.

On its Web site at <http://www.mentalhealth.org>, the United States Department of Health and Human Services has posted the following warning signs that may point to a possible mental health problem or serious emotional disturbance:

The following emotions and feelings are potential warning signs:

- Extreme anger, frequent crying, or overreaction to situations and events;
- Worthlessness or guilt;
- Anxiety or excessive worry;
- Long-term grief after a loss or death;
- Extreme fearfulness or excessive fear beyond most teens;
- Constant concern about physical problems or appearance; and
- Fear that his or her mind is controlled or is out of control (SAMHSA).

Adults should intervene if a teen:

- Performs poorly in school;
- Loses interest in things that are usually enjoyed;
- Has unexplained changes in sleeping or eating habits;
- Avoids friends or family and wants to be alone all the time;
- Daydreams too much and cannot get things done; or
- Feels that life is too hard to handle or talks about suicide (SAMHSA).

Adults should become concerned if the teen is limited by:

- Poor concentration and cannot make decisions;
- An inability to sit still or focus attention;
- Worry over being harmed, hurting others, or about doing something "bad";
- The need to wash, clean things, or perform certain routines dozens of times a day;
- Thoughts that race through his or her mind that are almost too fast to follow; and
- Persistent nightmares (SAMHSA).

Intervention is necessary if the teen:

- Uses alcohol or other drugs;
- Eats large amounts of food and then forces vomiting, abuses laxatives, or takes enemas to avoid weight gain;
- Continues to diet or exercise obsessively although the teen is too thin;
- Often hurts other people, destroys property, or breaks the law; or
- Does things that can be life threatening (SAMHSA).

Youth workers who suspect that an adolescent is suffering from mental health problems, or any of the issues addressed in this book, should follow established protocols and contact the responsible individual in the respective organization. Additional information about mental health warning signs is available on the National Mental Health Association's Web site at <http://www.nmha.org/infoctr/factsheets/11.cfm> or <http://psychology.about.com/library/weekly/aa093000b.htm>.

Part II: The Issues

Chapter Four

Maltreatment: Neglect and Abuse

Maltreatment of adolescents is on the rise—and startlingly so. In a country that is one of the most developed in the world, the amount of maltreatment is truly astonishing. The U.S. Advisory Board on Child Abuse and Neglect estimates that approximately 2,000 children die each year as a result of child abuse and neglect—that is five children every day.

One of the challenges in defining adolescent maltreatment is the widespread belief that teens have brought this on themselves because of the difficulty of their age.

> "It's okay, now, Marie. Go ahead and tell it. Then maybe someday other girls like you and me can fly through this stupid world without being afraid."—
> *I Hadn't Meant to Tell You This* by Jacqueline Woodson

"As a society, we tend not to have a sympathetic view of adolescents. We prefer to cast them as perpetrators, not as victims of crime and violence; as pursuers of risk, experimenting with drugs and sex, not as victims of abusive caregivers; as underachievers with no interest in the future, not as vulnerable youth suffering from low self-esteem and depression as a result of living with abuse" (U.S. Department of Health and Human Services, *Adolescent Maltreatment* 4). A second challenge is the definition of physical abuse, which focuses on the seriousness of the injury. Because teens are bigger and can fight back, they tend to receive less physical abuse than children. Whereas children are the recipients of physical abuse, teens are more likely to suffer emotional abuse. Few states have legal definitions of abuse that include standards of emotional and psychological harm (Powers and Jaklitsch 8).

A 1999 report authored by the National League of Cities and three other groups identified the 10 most critical threats to America's children. They consider child neglect and abuse to be one of the most formidable problems facing youth today. Neglected and abused children are more likely to experience juvenile crime, poor academic performance, drug and alcohol abuse, and domestic violence. These children are more vulnerable to low self-esteem, loss of trust, feelings of futurelessness, phobias, depression, and other psychiatric disorders

(Lowenthal 205). Adolescents who have been maltreated are at greater risk of depression and suicidal behavior. In addition, the romantic partners of maltreated adolescents are at substantial risk for dating violence because these adolescents are more likely to be aggressive (Wolfe et al. 282).

Maltreatment actually causes the brain to be diminished in capacity. Studies of adults who experienced continuous abuse as children indicate that the prolonged stress of maltreatment results in shrinkage of those areas of the brain responsible for memory, learning, and the regulation of affect and emotional expression. The brains of maltreated children can be 20–30% smaller than those of their non-maltreated peers (Perry 18). Abused and neglected children live under a state of constant alert which "may help them avoid further maltreatment, but it also degrades their development" and leads to emotional, behavioral, learning, and physical difficulties (Lowenthal 205).

While the causes of maltreatment are complex and interconnected, some experts blame the overall disintegration of the American family. Fifty percent of all marriages end in divorce. More and more children are being brought up in single-parent households and with nonbiological caretakers. A 1993 study conducted in Great Britain found that the safest environment for a child is living with both biological parents who have never been divorced; the least safe environment—which is 33 times more dangerous for the child—is living with the biological mother who is cohabitating with her boyfriend (Fagan 19).

In the 1993 Third National Incidence Study of Child Abuse and Neglect (NIS-3), the National Center on Child Abuse and Neglect found that the increase in maltreatment may be blamed on two other factors: parental use of illicit drugs and economics. Children whose parents use drugs and alcohol are more than three times as likely to be abused and four times as likely to be neglected than children whose parents do not use these substances (The National League of Cities et al., par. 53). Economics is a contributing factor because "family income is the strongest correlate of incidence in nearly all categories of abuse and neglect, with the lowest income families evidencing the highest rates of maltreatment" (U.S. Department of Health and Human Services Administration, *Executive Summary*, par. 72). Children and teens living in families with incomes under $15,000 per year were 22 times more likely to be victims of neglect than children in families with incomes over $30,000 (Marcynyszyn and Eckenrode 468).

Other findings of the NIS-3, which is considered to be the best resource for data on abused and neglected children, are:

- The number of physically neglected children increased 102% between the years 1986 (when the NIS-2 was released) and 1993. Not only have the number of incidents increased, but the injuries have become more serious;
- The number of sexually abused children increased during those years by 83%;
- The incidence of emotionally neglected children increased by 333%;
- There was a 43% increase in the number of physically abused children; and
- The only form of abuse or neglect that did not increase during the years between 1986 and 1993 was educational neglect (U.S. Department of Health and Human Services Administration, *Executive Summary*, par. 28).

As the above statistics indicate, abuse and neglect are significant problems in American society and are on the rise. Because many children and teens experience both parental abuse and neglect, it is important for educators to understand the definitions and symptoms of maltreatment in order to advocate for appropriate prevention and intervention measures.

Neglect is the most prevalent form of maltreatment facing American children and adolescents today (Marcynyszyn and Eckenrode 467). Neglect falls into three categories: physical, emotional, and educational. A simple definition of neglect is that children and teens are being neglected when they are not being adequately housed, clothed, or fed (Powers and Jaklitsch 11).

Physical neglect is the refusal to provide health care, delay in providing health care, abandonment, expulsion of an adolescent from home, inadequate supervision, failure to meet food and clothing needs, and failure to protect an adolescent from hazards (Abuse, par. 5). Teens who run away from home are not necessarily being temperamental and difficult; they are often "pushouts" or "throwaways." According to the National Runaway Switchboard, 1.3 million runaway and homeless youth are living on the streets of America, and one out of every seven children will run away before the age of 18. Runaways may be running from neglect and abuse, but they are often running to situations that put them at even greater risk of physical harm and emotional deprivation. Besides the fact that runaways are missing out on receiving an education, each year approximately 5,000 runaway and homeless kids die from assault, illness, and suicide (National Runaway Switchboard).

A second category of neglect—emotional—is a form of psychological abandonment. According to the NIS-3, the highest rates of emotional neglect occur during late childhood and adolescence, between the ages of nine and 17.

Emotional neglect is:

- The failure to nurture or provide affection to the child;
- Exposing a minor to severe and chronic spousal abuse;
- Permitting a teen to use alcohol or other controlled substances;
- Encouraging an adolescent to engage in antisocial, delinquent, or criminal behaviors; and
- Refusing to provide psychological care, delaying the provision of mental health care, and other forms of inattention (U.S. Department of Health and Human Services Administration, *Adolescent Maltreatment*, par. 16).

Educational neglect is associated with acts of omission and commission that permit chronic acts of truancy, failure to enroll the adolescent in school, and inattention to individual academic needs. Neglected adolescents may perform poorly in school, show deficits in cognitive and social-emotional functioning, and may appear socially withdrawn and passive (Marcynyszyn and Eckenrode 468).

When compared to other maltreated children, neglected children seem to have the most severe problems. Neglect appears to have a greater long-term impact on academic performance than does abuse. Neglected children and teens are the least successful on cognitive tasks and are more likely to be retained or referred for special education as a result of possible learning or social-emotional difficulties. They are more anxious, inattentive, and apathetic than other students. Socially, neglected children tend to exhibit inappropriate behaviors and are not accepted by their peers (Lowenthal 206).

Victims of neglect may display the following behaviors:

- They are often hungry and have no money for lunch;
- They may show signs of malnutrition;
- They are irritable;
- They show evidence of inadequate home management—they are unclean and unkempt, their clothes are torn and dirty, and they are often unbathed;
- They are in need of medical attention for such correctable conditions as poor eyesight, dental care, and immunizations;
- They do not display affection, humor, or joy; and
- They lack parental supervision (Squyres, Landes, and Quiram 12).

The second form of maltreatment is abuse. The three categories of abuse are: physical, sexual, and emotional. Physical abuse is injury inflicted by punching, beating, kicking, biting, burning, hair-pulling, shoving, or otherwise harming a child (Squyres, Landes, and Quiram 10). When discipline crosses the line and becomes too harsh, then it becomes abuse. Because of stress, parents may lose control and become abusive. According to Frank Putnam of the National Institute for Mental Health, abuse is "probably the single biggest factor for mental illness. It is worse than being born with two schizophrenic parents" (Strong 79). Teachers rate abused children as more overactive, inattentive, and impulsive than non-abused children; less motivated to achieve at school; and having more difficulty learning.

Adolescents who have been physically abused may display the following behaviors:

- Generalized anxiety;
- Depression;
- Adjustment and behavioral problems;
- Academic difficulties;
- Sleeping problems;
- Increased drug use;
- Self-destructive and reckless behaviors;
- Suicidal thoughts;
- Eating disorders;
- Violence against siblings, parents, and others;
- Fear of authority figures;
- Self-injury;
- Inability to concentrate; and
- Aggressive behavior (Physical Abuse, par. 3).

The definition of sexual abuse includes the fondling of a child's genitals, intercourse, incest, rape, sodomy, exhibitionism, and sexual exploitation. Sexual abuse is especially devastating to the developing psyche of the child. "Recurring sexual trauma, especially at the hands of a parent or other trusted loved one, is emotional terrorism of the highest order—so psychologically annihilating it has been called 'soul murder'" (Strong 65). If a stranger commits these acts, then it is called sexual assault. When these acts are committed by a caregiver (parent, babysitter, teacher, or day care provider) it is called sexual abuse. Usually the perpetrators of sexual abuse are known to the adolescent. Children and young adolescents between the ages of nine and 12 are at greatest risk for sexual abuse. Boys are at risk too, but they are less likely to report the abuse than girls. One severe consequence of sexual abuse is that it "can shatter a child's capacity for trust and intimacy" (Strong 67).

Sexually abused children may display the following behaviors:

- Unusual interest in or avoidance of all things of a sexual nature;
- Sleep problems or nightmares;
- Depression or withdrawal from friends or family;
- Seductiveness which may increase the risk of unintended pregnancy;
- Statements that their bodies are dirty or damaged;
- Eating disorders;
- Self-injury;
- Increased suicide attempts; and
- Increased risk of unintended pregnancy (Squyres, Landes, and Quiram 3).

Emotional or psychological abuse is a complex issue that has been gaining attention since the late 1980s. This type of abuse is very difficult to substantiate and corroborate because it does not leave physical evidence such as bruises and scars. It is difficult to define because of the existence of diverse cultural norms for acceptable and unacceptable parenting behavior; however, it is not a single occurrence but is repetitive and cumulative in nature. Experts believe that "children are thought to be psychologically and emotionally resilient to occasional inappropriate verbal or nonverbal acts" (Henry and Luster 254). Emotional abuse can be acts of commission as well as acts of omission. It is estimated that 6% of abuse and neglect cases substantiated nationally in 1997 fell into the category of emotional abuse. However, emotional abuse generally occurs along with other forms of abuse or neglect.

Six examples of emotional abuse are:

1. Spurning, which is verbal attacks, humiliation, and rejection;
2. Terrorizing, which is making threats to seriously harm or kill;
3. Observing family violence;
4. Exploiting and corrupting by encouraging engagement in antisocial or criminal behavior or encouraging a child to use drugs or alcohol;
5. Isolating a child so as to prevent him or her from interacting with peers or locking him or her within an enclosed area; and
6. Denying emotional responsiveness by being psychologically unavailable to the child, ignoring the child's attempts to interact with parents, or refusal to engage the child (Henry and Luster 275).

Adolescents who have been emotionally abused are more likely to engage in self-destructive, antisocial, and delinquent behaviors; to be diagnosed with a psychiatric disorder; to suffer from low self-esteem; and to either act out in aggressive ways or to withdraw. As children mature into adulthood they "may demonstrate signs of anxiety, depression, and dissociation" (Henry and Luster 256). The most critical element in healing emotionally abused children is the development of a positive and trusting relationship with a nurturing adult.

In a longitudinal study begun in 1970, a researcher in Israel compared a group of 28 abused children with a control group of 56 children who had not been abused

(Zimrin 341). The study found that the abused children were more likely than the non-abused children to suffer from:

- A passive attitude of acceptance, or fatalism, in which they feel that they can do "nothing to change their destiny or fight it in any way,"
- Feelings of being bad, stupid, and worthless because this is what they had heard from an early age;
- Aggression that sometimes leads to bullying and beating other children, or harming animals;
- Self-destructiveness which leads to self-harm or suicide;
- Difficulty in expressing emotions — "abused children are sad children: they lack the vitality, spontaneity, and gaiety that most children exhibit;" and
- Low cognitive achievement resulting from superficial relations with others, a low self-image, fatalism, and neglect by the environment. Sometimes educators may consider these children to be mentally deficient (343–345).

In addition, Zimrin found that abused children exhibited one of three behavioral patterns:

1. Yielding behavior characterized by introversion, passivity, and defeatism;
2. Pliable behavior characterized by a constant attempt to please others — these children were tolerant, appeasing, obedient, and attentive to the needs of others; and
3. Belligerent behavior characterized by constant demand for attention and by provocativeness — these children interfere, annoy, or hurt others (346).

Most of the damage caused by childhood abuse begins to be manifested during adolescence because "there is something about that developmental phase, the biochemical changes that are occurring, that starts to activate all the structural damage in the brain that comes from earlier trauma" (Strong 54). It is during adolescence that abused children begin to exhibit a number of acting-out and acting-in behaviors, from cutting and eating disorders to acts of outward aggression.

People who work with children need to learn how to recognize maltreatment and its consequences. Even though all states require educators to report suspected cases of abuse, a study reported in the *Harvard Education Letter* in 1995 found that 75% of educators could not identify or recognize abuse (Squyres, Landes, and Quiram 24).

Maltreatment Books for Middle School Readers

Buchanan, Jane. *Hank's Story.* **New York: Farrar, Straus and Giroux. 2001.**
Between 1854 and 1929, more than 150,000 orphaned and abandoned children in New York, Boston, and other cities in the east rode "Orphan Trains" to new lives in the Midwest. In this book, Hank and his brother ride the train to Nebraska only to find that they were better off on their own than with the mean and brutal Mr. and Mrs. Olson. For some maltreated children, school is a safe haven, but not for Hank at the Disappointment Creek School. Its teacher, Mr.

Givens, is demeaning and cruel to the orphans. Hank is bullied and prodded into fights with boys who have been abused themselves. Eventually Hank turns to Molly, a kindly older woman who takes care of wounded animals, and she intercedes to have him removed from the Olson's home. This middle school story deals with resilience, friendship, and the power of kindness.

Conly, Jane Leslie. *What Happened on Planet Kid.* **New York: HarperCollins Publishers. 2000.**
Set during a time when the Senators were the major league baseball team in Washington, D.C., this book chronicles the summer that Dawn spent with her aunt and uncle on their farm while her mother recuperated from knee surgery. Dawn, an avid baseball fan who harbors aspirations to play in the major leagues, makes friends with Charlotte, a local girl. Dawn soon learns that whenever things are not going well for Charlotte's father, he lets off steam by following the Biblical axiom: spare the rod and spoil the child. Because Dawn is sworn to secrecy, she does not tell anybody about what she has seen at Charlotte's house until she is safely home with her parents. Dawn decides to help Charlotte and her mother, brothers, and sisters escape their abusive situation by selling her beloved baseball card collection and sending the money to them. Dawn's father supports her decision and adds $100 to the $70 that she received from the sale of her baseball cards. Dawn is a strong-willed girl who knows how to make a difference.

Klass, David. *You Don't Know Me.* **New York: Farrar, Straus and Giroux. 2001.**
After John's father walks out on the family, his mother eventually falls in love with an abusive man who moves in with them. Soon the boyfriend starts beating John and forces him to become involved in a burglary ring. Told in diary format from a teen's point of view, *You Don't Know Me* is the story of the dangers that can befall a child when the mother brings a dangerous stranger into the home. John is at first unwilling to tell his mother about the beatings because he believes that she will side with the boyfriend. In the character of John, Klass communicates a teen's very real fear of being displaced by a boyfriend or new husband.

Konigsburg, e.l. *Silent to the Bone.* **New York: Atheneum Books for Young Readers. 2000.**
Branwell is accused of hurting Nikki, his baby half-sister, by dropping and shaking her — at least that is what the 911 recording indicates. After the accusation, Branwell stops talking, and it is up to Connor, his best friend, to investigate the truth. This mystery touches on the issues of child abuse, divorce, and a teen's infatuation with an older woman. In addition, teen readers will find comfort in this story as they realize that there are others like them who are trying to find their way in complicated families consisting of parents, step-parents, and half-siblings.

Reeder, Carolyn. *Foster's War.* **New York: Scholastic. 1998.**
Set in San Diego, this historical fiction book opens on the day Pearl Harbor was bombed. Foster has no idea that his world is about to change so dramatically.

Mel, Foster's oldest brother, has already run off to join the military to escape his father's demeaning words and actions. With Mel gone, Foster now takes the brunt of his father's short temper and prejudice. Soon Foster witnesses the prejudice and hatred toward Americans of Japanese descent as they are relocated to detention centers. Even though Foster's mother does her best to placate her husband, the children still suffer. Reeder has written a realistic book about children who must tiptoe around an abusive father.

Shaw, Susan. *Black-eyed Suzie.* **Honesdale, PA: Boyds Mills Press. 2002.**
Even though this book is about a 12-year-old middle school student who is viciously abused by her mother, the sophistication of the story and the writing style also make it suitable for high school collections. Although Suzie's family looks normal from the outside, something terrible has caused her to stop talking, walking, eating, and sleeping. By the time anyone takes notice, Suzie is practically catatonic. Suzie's mother tells the doctors that her daughter is only acting this way to embarrass the family for something that happened in the past. Suzie is taken to the St. Dorothy's Mental Hospital where she slowly recovers as she begins to feel safe and protected from her mother. Suzie only starts talking after her sister, Deanna, becomes the object of their mother's abuse.

Williams, Carol Lynch. *The True Colors of Caitlynne Jackson.* **New York: Bantam Doubleday Dell Books for Young Readers. 1997.**
Twelve-year-old Caity Jackson and her 11-year-old sister, Cara, have endured the rantings and ravings of their physically and emotionally abusive mother for what seems like forever. Even though many adults have heard the yelling and screaming and seen the bruises, they have never interceded. The girls have survived by sticking together and trying to outmaneuver their abusive mother. After their mother abandons them for the summer, Caity and Cara are mostly relieved and try to live as normal a life as possible by sleeping late, cooking whatever they want to eat, and swimming in the lake at midnight. But when the food and money run out, they know that they have to do something to save themselves.

Woodson, Jacqueline. *I Hadn't Meant to Tell You This.* **New York: Bantam Doubleday Dell Books for Young Readers. 1994.**
Marie and Lena have something in common: each has lost her mother. Written as a flashback, this is Marie's story about how she learns of Lena's sexual abuse and then tries to help her. Because Lena is afraid to shower or bathe at home for fear of attracting the sexual attention of her father, Marie invites Lena and her sister, Dion, over on Saturdays to wash in her bathtub. Before these bathtub "dates," Lena would go to school with greasy, matted hair even though she wanted to take pride in her appearance. The sequel, *Lena*, takes up where this book ends and is the story of the two sisters as runaways.

Maltreatment Books for High School Readers

Cole, Brock. *The Facts Speak for Themselves.* **Arden, NC: Front Street. 1997.**
A British study found that the children most in danger of abuse live with their mother and her live-in boyfriend. In this book, the reader will witness what happens to Linda, a 13-year-old girl, as a result of a selfish mother who is unaware of the impact that her drinking, neglect, moving, and numerous live-in boyfriends have had on her oldest child. This is a very raw and graphic book about Linda's life and the neglect and sexual abuse she endures. Linda's maltreatment culminates in a murder and suicide when her stepfather kills Linda's mother's boss who is sexually molesting her.

Crutcher, Chris. *Staying Fat for Sarah Byrnes.* **New York: Greenwillow Books. 1993.**
Sarah Byrnes is "truly one of the ugliest human beings outside the circus." Her severe neglect and abuse allow the reader to witness the horror and ridicule that Sarah Byrnes struggles with each and every day, and the resiliency that she develops in order to survive. Because Sarah Brynes' father is again threatening her life, she feigns a catatonic state in order to be sent to a psychiatric hospital until she can figure out her next move. In addition, you will read about kids who bully, taunt, and tease Eric and Sarah Byrnes, the abortion forced on a girl by a self-righteous preacher's son, and a wonderful teacher, Ms. Lemry, who helps these adolescents question and search for their own answers.

Deaver, Julie Reece. *The Night I Disappeared.* **New York: Simon Pulse. 2002.**
In this mysterious and eerie book, 17-year-old Jamie Tessman starts to disconnect from her world and falls into a trance-like dissociative state shortly after she moves to Chicago for the summer. Jamie's mother, a famous trial lawyer who works too many hours, is defending a teen, Sally Renfro, who is charged with the murder of her stepfather. This case causes Jamie to have strange dreams and to vaguely remember something that happened in her past. The reason for Jamie's dissociation becomes more apparent as the book progresses and her relationship with her mother is examined. *The Night I Disappeared* is a quick read and an interesting story that will appeal to young adults, especially those who have well-meaning but neglectful parents who are too involved in their careers.

Giles, Gail. *Shattering Glass.* **Brookfield, CT: Roaring Brook Press. 2002.**
Although this book has much bullying action that culminates in the baseball bat beating death of the class nerd, Simon Glass, it is a classic example of what can happen when parents emotionally neglect, sexually abuse, and bully their children. In *Shattering Glass*, Rob Hynes, the leader of the popular clique, who himself has been sexually abused, bullies and manipulates his peers until Simon Glass becomes popular and is expected to be crowned most popular during the homecoming dance. However, Simon uses his computer skills to rebel against Rob's control and manipulation by hacking into the school's computer program so that Rob wins the popularity contest instead. Simon's independence infuriates

Rob. What happens at the end of the book reflects the violence that may lie beneath the surface of students who have been abused and bullied.

Haddix, Margaret Peterson. *Don't You Dare Read This, Mrs. Dunphrey.* **New York: Simon & Schuster Books for Young Readers. 1996.**
Teens love reading journals and diaries, and *Don't You Dare Read This, Mrs. Dunphrey* will surely be consumed with gusto. This is Tish's journal written for Mrs. Dunphrey's English class. Because Mrs. Dunphrey will not read entries marked "Don't read this," most of Tish's entries are this type. The journal becomes cathartic as Tish's already chaotic home life takes a nose dive when her depressed mother becomes even more emotionally unavailable and neglectful, and eventually deserts her children to search for her cruel husband. Eventually Tish cannot cope anymore and asks Mrs. Dunphrey to read the journal. Mrs. Dunphrey then intervenes to help Tish and Matt reunite with their paternal grandparents. This strong high school story highlights the extent of many teens' problems and worries.

Levine, Gail Carson. "Pluto." *On the Edge: Stories at the Brink.* **Ed. Lois Duncan. New York: Simon & Schuster Books for Young Readers. 2000.**
Alicia, a junior in high school, has won the leading role in the senior class play. Her unresponsive parents do not realize she has talents because all their time is spent soothing Sara, the manipulative and difficult older sister who is constantly creating crises. Alicia thinks that if she became as difficult as Sara, then she might get more attention. By the end of this short story, Alicia realizes that she does not want Sara's role and is much happier being left alone. This story should be read by teens who feel that they do not get their fair share of parental attention.

Mazer, Norma Fox. *When She Was Good.* **New York: Arthur A. Levine Books. 1997.**
When She Was Good is told by Em, a teen who has survived her father's alcoholic rages, watched her mother fade away and die from depression, and endured her sister Pamela's physical and emotional violence. Em becomes a "throwaway" after her take-charge stepmother announces that Em is expected to drop out of school at 16 years of age and enter the workforce full-time. Not seeing much future in this situation, Em and Pamela run away. The lack of concern by the father is heartwrenching. Em's first person words are constantly interjected by the crude thoughts of her mentally ill sister. This book can be a springboard to *Ellen Foster* by Kaye Gibbons, an adult book about a young girl trying to maintain self-esteem in an abusive situation.

Nolan, Han. *Born Blue.* **New York: Harcourt, Inc. 2001.**
Janie, who changes her name to Leshaya, has lived a life of physical and emotional abuse as a result of her heroine-addicted mother who eventually places her in the foster care system and then sells her for drugs. In this complex story, Leshaya, who is white, identifies with African Americans because of Hanson, her best friend at the foster home. Because Leshaya lacks self-esteem, she has sex with an assortment of men as she pursues her dream of becoming a famous

(Lowenthal 205). Adolescents who have been maltreated are at greater risk of depression and suicidal behavior. In addition, the romantic partners of maltreated adolescents are at substantial risk for dating violence because these adolescents are more likely to be aggressive (Wolfe et al. 282).

Maltreatment actually causes the brain to be diminished in capacity. Studies of adults who experienced continuous abuse as children indicate that the prolonged stress of maltreatment results in shrinkage of those areas of the brain responsible for memory, learning, and the regulation of affect and emotional expression. The brains of maltreated children can be 20–30% smaller than those of their non-maltreated peers (Perry 18). Abused and neglected children live under a state of constant alert which "may help them avoid further maltreatment, but it also degrades their development" and leads to emotional, behavioral, learning, and physical difficulties (Lowenthal 205).

While the causes of maltreatment are complex and interconnected, some experts blame the overall disintegration of the American family. Fifty percent of all marriages end in divorce. More and more children are being brought up in single-parent households and with nonbiological caretakers. A 1993 study conducted in Great Britain found that the safest environment for a child is living with both biological parents who have never been divorced; the least safe environment—which is 33 times more dangerous for the child—is living with the biological mother who is cohabitating with her boyfriend (Fagan 19).

In the 1993 Third National Incidence Study of Child Abuse and Neglect (NIS-3), the National Center on Child Abuse and Neglect found that the increase in maltreatment may be blamed on two other factors: parental use of illicit drugs and economics. Children whose parents use drugs and alcohol are more than three times as likely to be abused and four times as likely to be neglected than children whose parents do not use these substances (The National League of Cities et al., par. 53). Economics is a contributing factor because "family income is the strongest correlate of incidence in nearly all categories of abuse and neglect, with the lowest income families evidencing the highest rates of maltreatment" (U.S. Department of Health and Human Services Administration, *Executive Summary*, par. 72). Children and teens living in families with incomes under $15,000 per year were 22 times more likely to be victims of neglect than children in families with incomes over $30,000 (Marcynyszyn and Eckenrode 468).

Other findings of the NIS-3, which is considered to be the best resource for data on abused and neglected children, are:

- The number of physically neglected children increased 102% between the years 1986 (when the NIS-2 was released) and 1993. Not only have the number of incidents increased, but the injuries have become more serious;
- The number of sexually abused children increased during those years by 83%;
- The incidence of emotionally neglected children increased by 333%;
- There was a 43% increase in the number of physically abused children; and
- The only form of abuse or neglect that did not increase during the years between 1986 and 1993 was educational neglect (U.S. Department of Health and Human Services Administration, *Executive Summary*, par. 28).

As the above statistics indicate, abuse and neglect are significant problems in American society and are on the rise. Because many children and teens experience both

Part II: The Issues

Chapter Four

Maltreatment: Neglect and Abuse

Maltreatment of adolescents is on the rise—and startlingly so. In a country that is one of the most developed in the world, the amount of maltreatment is truly astonishing. The U.S. Advisory Board on Child Abuse and Neglect estimates that approximately 2,000 children die each year as a result of child abuse and neglect—that is five children every day.

One of the challenges in defining adolescent maltreatment is the widespread belief that teens have brought this on themselves because of the difficulty of their age.

> "It's okay, now, Marie. Go ahead and tell it. Then maybe someday other girls like you and me can fly through this stupid world without being afraid."—
> *I Hadn't Meant to Tell You This* by Jacqueline Woodson

"As a society, we tend not to have a sympathetic view of adolescents. We prefer to cast them as perpetrators, not as victims of crime and violence; as pursuers of risk, experimenting with drugs and sex, not as victims of abusive caregivers; as underachievers with no interest in the future, not as vulnerable youth suffering from low self-esteem and depression as a result of living with abuse" (U.S. Department of Health and Human Services, *Adolescent Maltreatment* 4). A second challenge is the definition of physical abuse, which focuses on the seriousness of the injury. Because teens are bigger and can fight back, they tend to receive less physical abuse than children. Whereas children are the recipients of physical abuse, teens are more likely to suffer emotional abuse. Few states have legal definitions of abuse that include standards of emotional and psychological harm (Powers and Jaklitsch 8).

A 1999 report authored by the National League of Cities and three other groups identified the 10 most critical threats to America's children. They consider child neglect and abuse to be one of the most formidable problems facing youth today. Neglected and abused children are more likely to experience juvenile crime, poor academic performance, drug and alcohol abuse, and domestic violence. These children are more vulnerable to low self-esteem, loss of trust, feelings of futurelessness, phobias, depression, and other psychiatric disorders

Jazz singer. By the end of the story she finally makes peace with her AIDS ravaged mother and is able to break the cycle of abuse and neglect by leaving her child with Hanson and his educated African-American family.

Quarles, Heather. *A Door Near Here.* **New York: Laurel-Leaf Books. 1998.**
In this book, four children ranging in age from eight to 15 are doing their very best to hide the neglect they have endured ever since their mother lost her job and locked herself in her bedroom to drink. It is a somber story about the extraordinary measures taken by these children to protect their mother, keep the family together, and deflect the Division of Social Services away from their door step. In fact, neglect is the major reason that children are removed from a home in which parents have alcohol or other drug problems. While the children from the first marriage are living in poverty with their drunken and depressed mother, their dentist father, who senses that something is not right, has remarried and is driving a Porsche and taking vacations to Hawaii. This is a well-written and engaging story that feels real.

Rottman, S.L. *Hero.* **Atlanta: Peachtree Publishers. 1997.**
When confronted by Sean's confusion, anger, loneliness, fear, and stubbornness, many teachers would make him the topic of conversation in the faculty lounge, and he would be summarily dismissed with a "Whatever is going to happen to him?" comment. Teachers knew about his rotten home life, social workers had even been called, and Sean had repeatedly told his father—but nobody does anything. Sean is fortunate when he is sent to Mr. Hassler's farm to work off his community service hours. What brings new life to Sean is the birth of Knickers, a filly. What Knickers and Sean have in common is rejection by their mothers. Knickers will surely die unless someone else steps in to care for her. Sean takes the challenge because he knows what it is like to be neglected. This ia a well-crafted book that deals with some very tough issues about abuse, neglect, and the essence of being a hero.

Smith, Sherri L. *Lucy the Giant.* **New York: Delacorte Press. 2002.**
At well over six feet tall, Lucy Oswego is having a difficult time fitting into her Alaskan town of Sitka. Lucy had to grow up quickly after her mother ran away from home, leaving her with an alcoholic and neglectful father. When she finds a stray dog, Santa Barbara, her life begins to take on meaning. After Santa Barbara dies, partly because of her drunken father's refusal to help, she runs away and ends up on a crabbing boat in the Bering Sea. For the first time in Lucy's life she has found people who care for her. She wonders what her life would have been like if her father had not been an alcoholic and her mother had stayed. Teens who like nautical stories, such as *The Perfect Storm* by Sebastian Junger, will enjoy this book.

Sparks, Beatrice. ed. *Treacherous Love: The Diary of an Anonymous Teenager.* **New York: Avon Books. 2000.**
Jennie's life has become very complicated and sad ever since her father moved out and her depressed mother started taking pills to help her sleep. Jennie can't

believe her good luck when her dull math teacher, Miss Marress, is replaced by the handsome and energetic Mr. Johnstone. Almost immediately Mr. Johnstone senses that Jennie is very needy and he singles her out for special attention. One thing leads to another, and before long Mr. Johnstone is asking Jennie to meet him on the weekends so that they can spend time together. Mr. Johnstone, a sexual predator, plies her with alcohol and drugs, takes pornographic pictures of her, and rapes her. Only after Jennie realizes that she is being used does she tell her mother about Mr. Johnstone. Jennie is able to begin healing after her mother and father rally to her side.

Voigt, Cynthia. *When She Hollers*. New York: Scholastic Trade. 1994.
When She Hollers is one day in Tish's life—but what a day! This just happens to be the day that Tish takes charge and makes the transformation from victim to survivor. Tish arrives at the breakfast table wielding a knife and threatens to cut out her stepfather's heart if he ever sexually abuses her again. She spends the rest of this unsettling day looking for someone who will listen to her story. Finally she runs to her friend's father, a lawyer, who advises her about the legalities of sexual abuse. He encourages her to write down the entire story of her sexual abuse. Only then does she return home knowing that if her stepfather ever touches her again, she will have him arrested.

Chapter Five

Substance Abuse

Though some statistics show that drug use among adolescents is on the decline, millions of teens still use substances that are illegal to them — cigarettes, alcohol, and illicit drugs. Teens may use drugs because they are bored, hurt, stressed, insecure, or lonely. Teens say that drugs make them feel happier and less socially isolated or rejected, and relieve feelings of depression, low self-esteem, and anxiety (Ladd 727). Because teens consistently overestimate the amount of drug use, they may start using drugs to emulate their more popular peers whom they mistakenly believe are substance users (Huggins, par. 7).

Factors that place teens at risk for substance abuse are economic and social deprivation, availability of drugs, family history of alcoholism and parental drug use, academic failure and low commitment to school, friends who use drugs, and early first use of drugs (Indiana University 1). In the text, *Adolescence*, Steinberg identifies other factors that contribute to substance abuse problems. The first risk factor is adolescence, a "transition-proneness" time when teens are already more sensitive to influences around them (3). These influences may result in apathy and distancing from school and family. Researchers have found that the rate of drug and alcohol use tends to increase during adolescence and that teens become addicted to alcohol and drugs more quickly than adults (Hamilton, par. 1). The second risk factor is the personality and motivational characteristics of impulsivity, depression, anger, and low achievement which may make a teen more vulnerable to substance abuse. The third risk factor, family relationships, is critical because teens are at greater risk of using drugs if one or both parents are users (Steinberg 433). They are also at greater risk if their parents do not regularly talk to them about the dangers of drugs. Teens whose parents do are 42% less likely to use drugs. However, only one in four teens reports having these regular conversations with parents (*Alcohol Use Among Teens* 2).

> "When she met him his habit was a little pet, but now it was a horse that rode him."
> — *The White Horse* by Cynthia D. Grant

There is a wide disparity in the drugs teens use. The reason that some drugs are more widely used than others is the "perceived benefits and perceived risks that young people come to associate with each drug" (U.S. Department of Health and Human Services 4). Drugs become popular to teens when they believe that the drug will do for them what they want without great risk. Likewise, drugs may lose popularity with teens when there is a decrease in the perceived benefits and an increase in the perceived risks. For instance, the decrease in cocaine was largely precipitated by the widely publicized cocaine-related death of Len Bias, a National Basketball Association first-round draft pick. Bias' death was originally reported as resulting from his first experience with cocaine. This later turned out not to be the case, but the message had already "taken" (U.S. Department of Health and Human Services 14).

According to a 2001 report on adolescent drug use, ecstasy and steroids were increasing in use; heroin, alcohol, tobacco, LSD, inhalants, and crack and powdered cocaine were decreasing in use; and marijuana, hallucinogens other than LSD, narcotics other than heroin, amphetamines, methamphetamines, and the "club drugs"—Rohypnol, GHB, and Ketamine—were holding steady in popularity (U.S. Department of Health and Human Services 4).

The three most widely used drugs by teens are tobacco, alcohol, and marijuana. Cigarette smoking has been called the greatest preventable cause of disease and mortality in the United States (U.S. Department of Health and Human Services 32). Cigarette use has been declining among teens and there has been a gradual increase in both teen disapproval of tobacco and the perceived risk of this drug. Even so, cigarettes are very accessible, and each day nearly 4,800 teens smoke their first cigarette (American Lung Association, par. 4). In a 2002 telephone survey conducted between May 8th and June 23rd, 70% of the 14- to 17-year-olds said they could illegally purchase cigarettes within five blocks of their homes (Huggins, par. 13). Because teens who begin to smoke may continue this health hazard throughout life, it is extremely important to implement prevention programs starting in elementary school.

Alcohol kills 6.5 times more teens than all illicit drugs combined. Alcohol use is associated with the leading cause of death and injury among teens—automobile crashes. In a 1999 National Household Survey on Drug Abuse, 10.4 million teens aged 12 to 20 were consuming alcohol (Ladd 726). More than 40% of ninth graders, 55% of 12th grade girls, and 65% of 12th grade boys reported consuming one or more drinks in the previous month (Blum 290). Episodic or binge drinking is considered to be the most dangerous type of alcohol consumption (U.S. Department of Health and Human Services 30). Children who begin drinking before the age of 15 are four times more likely to develop alcoholism in adulthood than children who do not start drinking until the legal age of 21 (Alcohol and You, par. 3). Teens consume 1.1 billion cans of beer each year and drink 35% of all wine coolers sold in the United States ('Let's Draw the Line', par. 5). The highest levels of alcohol use are found among teens living in the suburbs: nearly one in five suburban teens reports drinking more than once a month (Blum and Rinehart 12).

Marijuana is the illicit drug most widely used by teens. According to the Federal Government's 2001 report, *Monitoring the Future: National Results on Adolescent Drug Use*, approximately 40% of 12th graders had used marijuana in the preceding 12 months. Since 1975, between 83% and 90% of seniors in every senior class that was surveyed have said that they could get marijuana fairly easily or very easily if they wanted. Fewer teens disapprove of marijuana now than they did in the early 1990s. These two reasons—availability and low disapproval rates—contribute to marijuana's high use rate (U.S. Department of Health and Human Services 8).

There are two ways to determine whether a teen is abusing drugs: first, through blood and urine testing; and second, by interviewing parents, teachers, and others regarding the history of the teen and his or her current behaviors. The following behaviors might indicate that a teen is using drugs:

- Secretive behaviors;
- A change in the teen's personality or friends;
- A loss of interest in what were once favorite activities;
- Difficulty concentrating;
- Deteriorating physical appearance and grooming;
- Associating with known substance abusers;
- Borrowing or stealing money;
- Possessing drug paraphernalia, even if the teen claims that it belongs to a friend (*Signs of Alcohol or Drug Use*, par. 4);
- Skipping school and arriving late for class; and
- Deteriorating health — many marijuana users often develop sinusitis, pharyngitis, bronchitis, and emphysema within a year of beginning use (Barrett, par. 7).

One factor that makes it difficult to identify substance abuse is that many teen drug users also suffer from mental illnesses, which can mask the symptoms of drug use. Depression, anxiety, schizophrenia, Attention Deficit/Hyperactivity Disorder, obsessive compulsive disorders, and Post Traumatic Stress Syndrome can cause teens to self-medicate themselves in order to feel better. The results of a study that evaluated more than 1,100 teens who were receiving substance abuse treatment found that 63% of these teens had a mental health disorder (Martin, par. 7).

Because adolescence is an important developmental stage in which many lifestyle decisions are being made, it is critical that teens receive timely substance abuse treatment. Otherwise, teens that use drugs may be side stepped from participating in and making these important decisions. Treatment options include inpatient hospitalization, outpatient treatment programs, day programs, and residential programs (Martin, par. 3).

The best way to prevent teens from abusing drugs is by offering effective prevention programs. The most effective prevention programs use the social-influence model which focuses on identifying and dealing with the social pressures related to drug use and increases drug awareness; addresses social factors, attitudes, and cultural influences; teaches drug resistance skills, life skills, and intervention techniques; and involves all members of the school and larger community. Programs should be health-based, long-term, and responsive to the changing cognitive, emotional, and social worlds of the teen (Packer 15). In addition, prevention must occur drug by drug because the perceived benefits and risks for each drug differs (U.S. Department of Health and Human Services 4). Successful curricula are characterized by the following:

- Helping students realize that substance use is not the norm for teens;
- Teaching social skills to increase a teen's ability to handle social situations without needing to rely on drugs;

- Teaching teens the skills to evaluate and resist external drug pressures of advertising, role models, and peer influences;
- Helping teens understand the risks and consequences, both short- and long-term, of substance abuse;
- Developing resiliency factors such as goal setting, mentoring, and academic success; and
- Teaching teens to resist drugs by participating in interactive techniques such as role-playing, simulations, brainstorming, small group activities, cooperative learning, and class discussion (Bosworth, par. 6).

One highly regarded program called "Project Alert" uses small-group activities, role-playing, scenarios, and discussion to help students recognize the internal and external pressures to use drugs. To understand the power of advertising, "students analyze what a tobacco or liquor ad is suggesting and then rewrite the ad to reflect what they know to be true about smoking or drinking" (Adair 45).

Methods that are patronizing, moralistic, and threatening are ineffective. Ineffective programs tend to be didactic and overly focused on presenting factual information about the legal, biological, and psychological effects of drugs. Teens are more likely to make responsible choices about alcohol and other drugs when they are presented with accurate information; nurtured, respected, and listened to; given clear, consistent expectations for behavior; exposed to positive role models; and rewarded for choosing to live drug-free (Packer 15).

Teachers exert a significant influence on students' attitudes, knowledge, and opinions. "Adults in schools need to model the social, decision-making, and communications skills taught in the curriculum" (Bosworth, par. 8). By setting high expectations, integrating prevention messages into the general curriculum and using literature to help teens to understand peer pressures and personal consequences of substance abuse, educators can establish a healthy school and community climate that communicates a concern for students and a disapproval of drugs.

Substance Abuse Books for Middle School Readers

DeFelice, Cynthia. *Death at Devil's Bridge*. New York: Farrar, Straus and Giroux. 2000.

Thirteen-year-old Ben Daggett, who lives on Martha's Vineyard, is spending the summer earning money by being first-mate on a charter fishing boat. Ben, on the first day of his job, is the first person to see the sunken red Porsche. The gossip around town is that the sunken car is somehow connected to drugs. Ben is thrilled when Donny, a local ultra cool drop-out, wants to hang out with him. It does not take Ben long to figure out that Donny is responsible for a series of break-ins and has something to do with the sunken car. Before long, Ben finds himself delivering drugs for Donny. Although Ben remembers that he was taught in drug awareness class to just say "No," he buckles the first time he is offered a drink. This book offers many opportunities to talk to teens about making good decisions and the difficulty of standing by them.

Koertge, Ron. *The Heart of the City*. New York: Orchard Books. 1998.
> This is an engaging, feel-good story about two middle school girls who save their multicultural and "rainbow" neighborhood in Los Angeles from being taken over by crack dealers and users. *The Heart of the City* shows readers that there are many ways to fight drugs and young teens can lead the effort. This story tackles the issues of diversity, racial intolerance, and how to fight back and make a difference using whatever talents one has—in this case, art.

Peck, Richard. *Strays Like Us*. New York: Dial Books. 1998.
> For teens like Molly and Will, who have had their families disrupted because of drugs, starting at a new school is one more thing to overcome. In this story, Molly must accept the fact that her addicted mother has left her and will not be coming back because the attraction to drugs is too great. Will's problem is that his father is dying from AIDS, which he contracted from a dirty needle. There is a scene in this book in which Will is thrown off the baseball team because the other players are afraid to play with him for fear he might be infected with the deadly virus. Luckily, both teens are able to bond with their grandparents and each other.

Substance Abuse Books for High School Readers

Anonymous. *Go Ask Alice*. Simon & Schuster Books for Young Readers. 1967.
> Even though this book was written over 30 years ago, *Go Ask Alice* still remains timely and engaging to teens because the language is not dated, and the story is believable. Written in diary format, *Go Ask Alice* is the actual story of a 15-year-old who gets hooked on drugs, runs away from home, and eventually dies of an overdose. The story is shocking because of the speed at which Alice becomes part of the drug culture and becomes dependent on drugs. The message in this book for adults is never underestimate the power of peer influence or the enticement of drugs.

Burgess, Melvin. *Junk*. Adapted for the stage by John Retallack. London: Methuen Publishing, Ltd. 1996.
> *Junk* is the stage adaptation of Burgess's book *Smack*. In this two act play, readers look into the lives of Tar and Gemma, two runaways who have become hooked on heroin. What is alarming about *Junk* and *Smack* is the speed at which these teens become addicted to drugs, and how quickly their lives spiral downward into crime and prostitution. For more complete information about the storyline, read the review below about *Smack*. The story and language in *Junk* and *Smack* are very graphic.

Burgess, Melvin. *Smack*. New York: Avon Tempest. 1996.
> Set in Great Britain during the mid-80s, *Smack* is the American release of *Junk*, a story about love birds Tar and Gemma who run away from home. They meet up with a group of people who welcome them into their squat—an English term meaning a vacant house that is taken over by homeless people who set up

residence. At first, the freedom to drink and smoke marijuana is riveting. Soon, however, they need stronger drugs to give them the same rush. This book gives the reader a very ugly glimpse into a community of teens as they become more dependent on drugs, are drawn into prostitution, and give birth to babies who are junkies. Burgess calls this book faction—truth that has been fictionalized.

Glovach, Linda. *Beauty Queen.* **New York: HarperCollins Publishers. 1998.**
Mature students who have read and enjoyed *Go Ask Alice* might want to migrate to *Beauty Queen*, which is a much more grown-up and gritty version of *Alice*. Instead of the 14- or 15-year-old school girl in *Go Ask Alice*, Sam, the main character in *Beauty Queen*, is a 19-year-old who is working a dead end, minimum wage job at a fast food restaurant. She hears that she can make more money dancing topless. Because she never before has done this type of thing and is very nervous to be dancing around so skimpily-clad, she starts taking heroin—just a little bit—to calm her down. In this hard-edged book, Sam, like Alice, starts off believing that she will not become addicted but soon succumbs to the drug and the accompanying lifestyle. Told in diary format, this book is for only the most mature high school students.

Grant, Cynthia D. *The White Horse.* **New York: Simon Pulse. 2000.**
The White Horse, a book about an extraordinarily dysfunctional family, is told in three points of view: the past in which Raina writes for her creative writing teacher because she cannot talk about the abuse; the present in which Raina tells about her life as a throwaway teen who becomes pregnant; and the present perspective of Margaret Johnson, a discouraged teacher who gets little support in her work with severely troubled teens. This book could be used on many levels to discuss such issues as pregnancy, neglect and maltreatment, and substance abuse. Teachers will especially relate to Johnson's chapters and her many attempts to help throwaway and abused teens such as Raina. Eventually, Mrs. Johnson is able to dissuade Raina from raising her baby, and she adopts both Raina and the baby.

Keizer, Garret. *God of Beer.* **New York: HarperCollins Publishers. 2002.**
Beer. Kyle's life changes forever after he speaks that one word in Mr. Whalen's senior social studies class at Willoughby Union High School. *The God of Beer* is a witty and readable story about a group of seniors who promote the Great Beer Rebellion to protest the legality of the liquor laws, to try to lower the drinking age, and to destroy the exaggerated status of drinking. This book raises an interesting question about whether these laws actually encourage drinking by making alcohol more desirable. Adults will be struck by how accessible alcohol is and how much it is used by teens in this book—and many of these teens are leaders in the school. A great read for teens and adults alike who want to explore alcohol use by teens today.

Thomas, Rob. *Rats Saw God.* **New York: Simon & Schuster Books for Young Adults. 1996.**
Someone has to nominate Mr. DeMouy, a guidance counselor at Wakefield High School in San Diego, for the Guidance Counselor of the Year Award for recog-

nizing that something must have happened to Steve York to change him overnight from an A student and Merit Finalist to a student at risk of not graduating from high school. Knowing that there must be a reason and that reflection and journals are healing, DeMouy allows Steve to earn his English credit by writing a 100-page paper on the topic of his choice. After a shaky start, Steve decides to write about his parents' divorce, his father's constant disapproval and pressure on him to succeed, and the breakup of his first romantic relationship. *Rats Saw God* provides a glimpse into the drinking, drug, and sexual patterns of high school students who are not in the popular clique.

Chapter Six
Depression and Suicide

According to the Substance Abuse and Mental Health Services Administration, one in eight teens suffers from clinical depression, a serious emotional and mental disorder that is potentially life-threatening. Teen girls are more vulnerable to depression than are teen boys. Hispanic and African-American teens are more likely to have felt sad or hopeless than white students (Teenhealth, par. 3). "The peak time for risk of depression is around the ages of 13 and 14" with girls being more susceptible than boys (Koplewicz 81). Among teens, an episode of depression usually lasts from seven to nine months. Well over half of all depressed teens have a recurrence within seven years (Watkins, *Child and Adolescent Depression*, par. 1).

Depression is identified in terms of emotional, cognitive, motivational, and physical symptoms (Kenny 205). Emotional symptoms include sadness, anger, irritability, crying, feeling unloved and sorry for oneself, and a loss of humor.

Cognitive symptoms include difficulty concentrating and making decisions, a preoccupation with death, and a tendency to blame oneself when things go wrong. Motivational symptoms include withdrawal from contact with friends and family members and a loss of interest in school achievement. Physical symptoms include chronic tiredness, changes in appetite and sleep patterns, and increased aches and pains. Teens may be suffering from depression if they experience frequent lightheadedness, stomach pains, headaches, vomiting,

> "People who have never come close to seeking death don't understand its promise of an end to life's struggles. They don't understand the precarious teeter-totter on which a suicidal person balances, shuffling reasons to live and reasons to die back and forth to avoid hitting bottom. They don't understand that when you're that low, when you can't see beyond yourself and your fallen-apart world, it's the little things that send you over the edge, not the big things."—
> *Aimee* by Mary Beth Miller

and menstrual pains (NAMI Anxiety, par. 1). Depressed teens may become either hyperactive or lethargic.

Despite some similarities, symptoms of depression in teens differ from those experienced by depressed adults. Depressed teens are more likely to exhibit anxiety and fear of separation and meeting people than depressed adults. In addition, physical symptoms such as stomachaches, headaches, and psychosomatic complaints are far more common in depressed teens (*Health Net News*, par. 10). Depressed teens are more likely than depressed adults to overeat and gain weight, sleep too much, and become lethargic. Unlike depressed adults, teens do not show a drop in libido. They may continue to date and go to parties because depressed teens are able to temporarily react to their environment and not appear depressed. The teen may seem happy at a party even though he or she is very depressed (Koplewicz 18).

Most teens experience some depressive symptoms once in a while. The rate of depressive symptoms grows steadily throughout childhood. When asked if either they or a friend or acquaintance had experienced depression, 17% of 11- and 12-year-olds replied that they had. That number jumped to 42% for 15- to 17-year-olds (National Poll, par. 7). Girls are more likely to experience depression than boys, but the reason is not fully known. Researchers, however, point to stress as the likely cause. They say that the many changes teens experience as they move from childhood through adolescence are sources of stress that can lead to depression (Kenny 207). One source of stress is the transition from the protected elementary school to a middle school environment which brings more difficult academic work and the need to work with a variety of teachers—rather than one. Other stressors are physical and hormonal changes. Girls who mature early are especially vulnerable. Early maturing girls may develop friendships with older teens, who then introduce them to situations that they are not ready to handle. Society's emphasis on being thin causes some girls to become anxious about the weight gain that naturally accompanies puberty. As a result, teen girls may develop negative feelings about their bodies (Kenny 207).

Social scientists believe that there is a genetic predisposition to depression. "Statistically, children of depressed parents are three times more likely to become depressed themselves than children whose parents do not have depression" (Koplewicz 82). A study of 79 high school seniors by Field, Diego, and Sanders found that teens who were depressed were more likely to have a depressed or stressed parent (494). When the genetic risk interacts with life stress, depression may be the result (Kenny 207). "Some [researchers] feel that children inherit a predisposition to depression and anxiety, but that environmental triggers are necessary to elicit the first episode of Major Depression" (Watkins, *Child and Adolescent Depression*, par. 3).

Depressed teens tend to have fewer friends, spend less time doing homework, have a lower grade point average, exercise less, and report more marijuana and cocaine use than non-depressed teens (Field, Diego, and Sanders 491). Teens who are depressed may use drugs to make themselves feel better. Because exercise increases serotonin, the body's natural antidepressant, Field, Diego, and Sanders recommend that schools increase physical education programs as a way to lessen the symptoms of depression (498). In addition, depressed teens often suffer from one or more major psychiatric illnesses. Anxiety disorder, substance abuse, and Attention Deficit/Hyperactivity Disorder are frequently associated with teen depression (Watkins, *Child and Adolescent Depression*, par. 5).

Whether or not stressors or challenges set off a bout of depression may depend on how prepared teens are to deal with stress. Many of the positive and negative coping strategies that teens rely on to respond to life's challenges are learned in the home. When these coping strategies are not learned, teens may be unprepared to handle stressful situations. It may be necessary for educators and youth workers to teach teens to reach out for help. They can help teens to learn how to problem solve and cope with stress in positive ways rather than blaming themselves or using drugs or alcohol (Kenny 208).

Depression is a serious problem that calls for prompt and appropriate treatment. Sometimes teens act in belligerent, irritable, and hostile ways that are labeled "normal teen" behavior. These behaviors may indeed be the growing pains of adolescence when they are isolated events that occur for a short period of time. However, when these behaviors extend beyond a six-month period and seem "intractable and entrenched," treatment is needed. Four of the most common types of treatment are: psychotherapy in which teens explore events and feelings that are painful to them; cognitive-behavioral therapy to help teens change negative patterns of thinking and behavior; interpersonal therapy to focus on how to develop healthier relationships at home and at school; and medication such as Paxil, Effexor, and Prozac that may relieve the symptoms of depression (National Mental Health Association, par. 10; Koplewicz 265–275).

Feelings of depression may lead to suicide. Suicide is the third leading cause of death among those who are 15 to 24 years of age. It is the fourth leading cause of death among young teens aged 10 to 14 years. In 1997, more teens died from suicide than AIDS, cancer, heart disease, birth defects, and lung disease combined (Watkins, *Suicide*, par. 1).

Suicidal behavior is very complex and can be defined as thoughts, verbalizations, or actions intended to cause one's own death. Suicidal behavior extends along a continuum from ideation—thoughts or verbalizations about suicide—to actual completion. Suicide ideation is very common in the general adolescent population (Gallagher 732). Firearms, hanging, and gassing are the most common methods of completed suicide. Males tend to use more violent and lethal means, such as firearms and hanging. The methods that girls invoke are intentional overdose, wrist cutting, and gassing (735).

A previous suicidal attempt must be taken seriously because it is the biggest predictor of future attempts. Once a teen attempts suicide, statistics show that about one-half will eventually try again. Common risk factors for suicide are substance abuse; major depression with feelings of low self-esteem, helplessness, hopelessness, and loneliness; a sense of guilt; poor impulse control; and chronic difficulty with authority. Among girls, the most significant risk factor for suicide is depression followed by previous suicide attempts. For boys, a previous suicide attempt is the most significant predictor. Almost all teen suicide victims have suffered from psychiatric disorders such as depression, conduct disorders, antisocial personality disorders, Attention Deficit/Hyperactive Disorder, or substance abuse (Gallagher 735). In general, teen girls are more likely to attempt suicide, but boys are about four times more likely to succeed. Homosexual and lesbian teens are at greater risk for depression and suicide (734).

Teen suicide is not an impulsive act. Most teens who attempt suicide have communicated clear messages about their intent. Suicides follow a pattern that includes three elements. First, there exists either a history of problems, or a long-term problem. Problems can include losing a parent through death or divorce, living in a family with considerable discord, being a victim of child abuse, or living with an alcoholic in the family. Hyperactivity or undiagnosed learning disabilities also pose serious long-term problems for adolescents. Second, the problem is compounded by stress. Long-term problems can cause teens to become socially isolated, perform poorly in school, and miss school. Third, suicide often occurs after a precipitating event, such as a family crisis, a significant personal loss or disappointment, or an upset to self-esteem. Upsets include failing a course, losing one's place on a sports team, or being fired from a part-time job. The anniversary of a loss can also provoke a suicide attempt (Teenhealth, pars. 8–9).

Suicide prevention programs may be very beneficial in raising awareness about the problem of teen suicide. One program, "Red Flags," for middle and high school-aged students, is funded by the Ohio Department of Education to teach students, teachers, and parents about depression and suicide. A therapist works with any teen who self-identifies symptoms of depression. Teachers receive in-service training to prepare them to introduce materials about depression to their classes (*Ohio's Mental Health*, par. 3).

Other steps that can be taken by educators to prevent suicides are:

- Report concerns to the proper school and district personnel as established by procedures and policies;
- Do not ignore a student who seems depressed as he or she might interpret this as not caring;
- Show concern for the student;
- Do not make promises of confidentiality to the student because an educator must alert the proper authorities if he or she suspects suicidal ideation;
- Pay attention to all references of suicide—even if made in a joking manner; and
- Be especially cautious if a student seems to snap out of a depression—just before attempting suicide, it is common for teens to appear more at peace because they have made the decision that ending their lives is a solution to their problems (Teenhealth, par. 10).

Depression and Suicide Books for Middle School Readers

Fields, Terri. *After the Death of Anna Gonzales*. New York: Henry Holt and Company. 2002.

Forty-seven of Anna's fellow students and teachers tell what it is like for them in the aftermath of her suicide. Their reactions in poetry range from "Why did Anna have to kill herself now? I don't mean to be rude or anything, but she certainly didn't have any consideration. Everyone knows how important this pep assembly is going to be" (52) to "The game doesn't always go your way. Forget fair. Feel forgotten. But damn it, Anna, You don't stop playing" (7) to "And I am forever left to wonder, whether telling you how truly special you were, might have made a difference" (67). This book is recommended for both middle and high school collections.

Irwin, Cait. *Conquering the Beast Within: How I Fought Depression and Won … And How You Can, Too.* **New York: Three Rivers Press. 1998.**
This is the true-life account of Cait Irwin's depression that began when she was 13 years old. Her instructive story is told in a fairy tale format. Depression is characterized as the Wolf who does all it can to ruin the lives of teens by destroying self-esteem. Irwin explains how symptoms of confusion, physical aches and pains, and loss of sleep can be blamed on the Wolf. She writes that depression—like a broken leg—takes time to heal and treatments such as therapy and medicine are required. Irwin relates her experience with depression in such a way that this book is a must buy for both middle and high school collections. The book also includes letters written by Irwin's relatives who describe their experience with her depression.

Depression and Suicide Books for High School Readers

Dewey, Jennifer Owings. *Borderlands.* **New York: Marshall Cavendish. 2002.**
As a result of an abusive father and a mother who stood by and watched, Jamie becomes depressed, attempts suicide by overdose, and is consequently hospitalized. Years of abuse have left Jamie feeling hopeless and unloved. During her stay in the psych ward, Jamie watches as a beautiful girl "with unblemished skin, long, black hair" dies of an overdose and wonders, "What had driven her to it? What dread convinced her it was time?" (16). She develops a close friendship with Adam, a teen who experiences severe psychotic episodes. During one episode, Adam jumps off a three-story building breaking many bones in his body. Adam's attention and friendship are healing because Jamie has never had caring people around her who were not paid to be nice to her. Each chapter contains flashbacks and insights into Jamie's life which help readers understand how a teen could become so desperate.

Draper, Sharon M. *Tears of a Tiger.* **New York: Atheneum. 1994.**
The obituary read: "Teen Basketball Star Killed in Fiery Crash. Nov. 8—Robert Washington, age 17, captain of the Hazelwood High School basketball team, was killed last night in a fiery automobile accident on I-75. Witnesses say the car, driven by Andrew Jackson, 17, also of the Hazelwood team, had been noticeably weaving across the lanes of the expressway just before it hit a retaining wall and burst into flames" (1). Even though it was Robert who died that night, a second victim, Andy, will die within months. Andy's overwhelming guilt and shame will cause him to place a gun to his head and pull the trigger. *Tears of a Tiger* traces Andy's reaction to the crash through police interviews, letters, articles, homework assignments, and conversations. The unfortunate lesson to learn is that Andy may not have died if only his parents, teachers, and friends had recognized the symptoms of depression and suicide and intervened on his behalf.

Mickle, Shelley Fraser. *The Turning Hour.* **Montgomery, AL: River City Publishing. 2001.**

The Turning Hour is a compelling story about a teenager's recovery from attempted suicide. One element that makes this book so interesting to read is its unusual point of view: the chapters alternate between the mother and the daughter who tell this story from their own perspectives. Their viewpoints draw readers into the story and provide insight into the complicated family dynamics that led to the teen's attempted suicide. Readers will not easily forget the "ah hah" moment when they discover the incident that caused her to want to end her life. This book should be read by mothers and daughters who want to delve into the effects of divorce and the consequences of lack of communication.

Miller, Mary Beth. *Aimee.* **New York: Dutton Books. 2002.**

This engaging story is a must read for all adults who care about teens and for teens who have depressed and suicidal friends. The message in this book that is so eloquently delivered is the need for parents and adults to be available to help teens with problems that they do not have the maturity to solve. If the adults in this book had been emotionally and physically available, then Aimee would still be alive today. Because parents would not listen, Zoe tried to handle Aimee's depression all by herself. As a result, when Aimee does commit suicide, Zoe is tried for murder. This book is told from two points of time—flashbacks and the present—and is written in Zoe's voice.

Powell, Randy. *Three Clams and an Oyster.* **New York: Farrar, Straus and Giroux. 2002.**

Three high school students are in the process of selecting Cade Savage's replacement on their four man flag football team. Ever since Cade has started drinking and using drugs, he has become useless to the team. The reason Cade starts using drugs is because he feels responsible for the death of Glen Como, the previous oyster of the team, who died as a result of their horsing around. Now it is Cade who wishes that he had died instead of Glen. After interviewing several candidates to replace Cade, the remaining three players on the four man flag football team decide on an athletic girl, Rachel Summerfield.

Rivers, Karen. *Surviving Sam.* **Vancouver: Polestar Books. 2001.**

Almost three years after Sam's death, his twin sister, Pagan, is still haunted by his death. Even now, she can still feel, hear, and see the avalanche that killed Sam and changed her life forever. *Surviving Sam* is Pagan Riddler's story of depression, suicide attempts, and self-harm. Even though the accident almost destroys the entire family, it is Pagan who is the most affected. This story has a strong message of hope and renewal as Pagan eventually is able to come out of her depression with the help of counseling and medication. The first indication that Pagan will survive is when she starts riding her bicycle again. A secondary issue is the homosexuality of one of Sam's friends. Teens grappling with sexual orientation issues may be more at risk for depression and suicide.

Sparks, Beatrice. *Jay's Journal.* **New York: Pocket Books. 1979.**

This is another book in the "Anonymous" series by Sparks that includes *Go Ask Alice*. Written in diary format, the topic of this book is witchcraft and suicide. The more Jay becomes involved in witchcraft and Satan worship, the more dependent on drugs he becomes. Soon his behavior is erratic and he believes that his friends are using voodoo on him so that he will not leave the coven. When Jay comes to believe that his only way out is to commit suicide, he shoots himself in the head. Even though this book has an older copyright, it may be of interest to librarians and media specialists looking for fiction books on witchcraft.

Wild, Margaret. *Jinx.* **New York: Walker & Company. 2002.**

After Jen's boyfriends die she decides to change her name to Jinx to match what her schoolmates are calling her. Told in narrative poetry, this story is about Jen's own confusion and pain caused by the desertion of her father and stepfather and her first boyfriend's suicide. Jinx delves into the impact that Charlie's suicide has on her and his family.

Chapter Seven
Eating Disorders and Body Image

Eating disorders are a serious and complex mixture of social, psychological, and physical problems that most often begin during the period between early adolescence and early adulthood. The American Psychiatric Association characterizes Anorexia Nervosa and Bulimia Nervosa as biopsychosocial disorders that result in distortions of self-image and self-perception (Thomsen, Weber, and Brown 3).

> "Today's my half birthday. It's the first day of summer, and I'm exactly eleven and a half. I usually make a wish on my birthdays, so I was thinking that I'd wish to be the thinnest girl at school, or maybe even the thinnest eleven-year-old on the entire planet..."—
> *Stick Figure* by Lori Gottlieb

According to the National Association of Anorexia Nervosa and Associated Disorders (ANAD), 10% of eating disorders develop in children 10 years old and younger, 33% develop between 11 and 15, and 43% develop between 16 and 20 (ANAD, *Facts*, par. 2). Young women are nine to 10 times more likely to be diagnosed with an eating disorder than are young men (Chaves 247). Eating disorders are most commonly found among white, middle-income or affluent intact families but can occur in all socioeconomic groups. ANAD's 1990 study of students at 20 high schools in 18 states found that 11% of the teens surveyed had Anorexia Nervosa or Bulimia Nervosa (ANAD, *High School Study*, par. 1).

The factors that place teens at risk for eating disorders are personality characteristics, family dynamics, stressful events, genetic and biological conditions, and the media (Chaves 250). Individuals with eating disorders tend to exhibit certain personality traits. For instance, anorexics tend to be high achievers, anxious, fearful, perfectionists, compliant, and insecure. Some anorexic teens may suffer from depression and obsessive-compulsive personality traits. Bulimics tend to be impulsive and view themselves as out of control. Families that are authoritative, lack nurturance and empathy, and promote thinness may cause daughters to rebel by controlling their own food intake. Some eating disorders are triggered by stressful events such as sexual abuse or going away to college.

Chemical abnormalities in the brain, specifically changes in the neurotransmitters, serotonin, and norepinephrine, have been found in teens with Anorexia Nervosa (Pruitt 262). Some teens with a strong commitment to athletics, such as dance and ballet, gymnastics, wrestling, and ice skating, may develop eating disorders as a way to achieve and maintain the ideal body shape or size. As they enter adolescence, many teen girls tend to perform more poorly in school, undergo a decline in their self-concept, and experience greater stress. They are twice as likely as boys to be depressed and they attempt suicide four or five times more often. This general decline in self-concept and depression puts teen girls at great risk for eating disorders (Rothenberg, par. 1). The timing of sexual maturation has an impact on eating disorders, too. Early maturing girls naturally become larger and curvier before their peers. They may feel fat and turn to unhealthy dieting practices to counteract these natural changes ("Timing of Menarche," par. 5).

Many mental health experts point to the "girl-poisoning" culture that communicates to teens that the road to happiness is via thinness and beauty (Pipher 12). Researchers believe that the negative impact of reading beauty and fashion magazines has led "many young women to internalize and embrace the sociocultural 'thin ideal' and, in turn, motivates them to attain it, sometimes through unhealthy dieting practices" (Thomsen, Weber, and Brown 2). Body image is a learned perception. More than 6.5 million adolescent females who read fashion magazines like *Seventeen* and *Teen* are internalizing the message that thinness and beauty lead to happiness. Thomsen, Weber, and Brown surveyed 502 high school women and statistically determined that reading fashion magazines encouraged anxiety about weight, which led to using anxiety suppressants or weight control pills (5). One popular teen magazine, *YM*, recognized the danger in communicating a message about extreme thinness and has elected not to print stories on dieting. Their editors are under strict orders not to show emaciated-looking models in the magazine and to include larger models in the magazine's stories (*YM*).

Anorexia Nervosa is one of the most common psychiatric diagnoses in young women. However, once entrenched, it is very difficult to treat, and "of all the psychiatric disorders, it has the highest fatality rate" (Pipher 174). Even though this eating disorder is defined as a loss of appetite, the victims actually deny their appetites despite feelings of constant hunger (Chaves 247). Anorexics restrict food as a means of gaining control over some aspect of their lives in a world where they feel powerless. Anorexia Nervosa is characterized by the maintenance of a minimal body weight which is less than 85% of expected weight, intense fear of weight gain despite being underweight, denial that the sufferers have a problem, and the loss of three consecutive menstrual cycles in post menarcheal women (Chaves 247). Pipher writes that dutiful daughters and high achievers are most at risk (174). Anorexia begins with dieting because the teen believes that her life will be better if she loses weight; but then the diet takes on a life of its own. She becomes obsessed with staying thin and not gaining weight. Anorexics have a tremendous fear of becoming fat and losing control over the amount of food that is eaten (National Eating Disorders Association, *Anorexia Nervosa*, par. 1).

According to ANAD, the warning signs of Anorexia Nervosa are dramatic weight loss, preoccupation with food and weight, anxiety about getting fat, denial of hunger, and excuses to avoid mealtimes or situations involving food. When they do eat a meal with the family, anorexics will play tricks, such as pushing their food around to make it look like they have eaten more than they really have. Health consequences of this illness are weight loss, fatigue, weakness and fainting, dehydration, abnormally slow heart rate, and low blood pressure, which could lead to heart failure, and the growth of a downy layer of hair called "lanugo" on the face and body. The purpose of "lanugo" is to keep the body warm (ANAD, *Warning Signs*).

Bulimia Nervosa, the most common eating disorder among young females, involves repeated episodes of binge eating, which are followed by compensatory behaviors of self-induced vomiting, fasting, misuse of laxatives or diuretics, and/or excessive exercise. Between 1% to 4% of adolescent and young women are bulimics (Bulimia Nervosa, par. 4). Eighty percent of bulimics are female. When a bulimic is around others she may appear to eat normally; but when alone, she will binge and purge. Binges, which may last anywhere from several minutes to several hours, occur in secrecy and are characterized by lack of control. After a binge, bulimics tend to feel depressed, self-critical, and shameful. They engage in the compensatory behaviors mentioned above as a means of not gaining weight, relieving physical discomfort, and easing stress (Chaves 248).

Bulimics tend to have a more accurate perception of body weight and shape than anorexics. Bulimics may appear healthier, but this disease can also have serious life-threatening health consequences (Pipher 169). They are more likely than anorexics to acknowledge that they have a problem and seek help. Bulimics are the ultimate people pleasers. Most are attractive with good social skills. According to Pipher, they are "cheerleaders and homecoming queens, the straight-A students and pride of their families" (170). Bulimics may use food to satisfy their inner needs. They purge as a means of achieving temporary control.

Evidence of binge eating is the disappearance of large amounts of food in short periods of time. Further evidence of purging includes frequent trips to the bathroom, signs and smells of vomiting, the presence of wrappers or packages of laxatives or diuretics, an excessive and rigid exercise regime, unusual swelling of the cheeks and face area, calluses on the backs of hands and knuckles from self-induced vomiting, and discoloration or staining of the teeth (ANAD, *Warning Signs*).

Bulimia can lead to physical complications, such as abdominal pain and a ruptured stomach, dehydration and loss of potassium and sodium from the body, which may lead to electrolyte imbalances, irregular heartbeats and heart failure, swollen salivary glands, fatigue, tooth and gum erosion, menstrual irregularity, and broken blood vessels in the eyes (*Bulimia Nervosa*, par. 2).

Treatment of eating disorders can be expensive and includes individual, group, and family therapy, medication, nutritional counseling, support groups, and self-help groups (Chaves 251). According to the National Association of Anorexia Nervosa and Associated Disorders, only about 50% of anorexics can be cured (ANAD, *Facts*, par. 3). The longer the eating disorder continues, the more difficult it is to treat.

Educators and parents must devise strategies to counteract the media messages of thinness and beauty and help improve teens' body image. Educators can develop eating disorder prevention efforts similar to substance abuse programs to reduce girls' perceptions of the importance of their appearance as well as addressing eating irregularities ('Certain Behaviors,' par. 2). Educators should become good role models about body image by following some of these guidelines:

- Do not talk negatively about your own body;
- Do not lose or gain weight dramatically;
- Do not utilize fad diets; and
- Model healthy exercise behavior (National Eating Disorders Association Prevention Guidelines).

Educators can use media literacy techniques to encourage teens to discuss the reality of fashion and beauty advertisements and the impact of these on their own body image.

Eating Disorders and Body Image Books for Middle School Readers

Frank, Lucy. *I Am An Artichoke.* **New York: Bantam Doubleday Dell Books for Young Readers. 1995.**
Spending the summer being a mother's helper in New York City seems like a dream come true to this 15-year-old girl who has always felt like an outsider in her own family. Within hours of starting this job, Sarah learns that Emily, the 12-year-old she has been hired to befriend, is going to be more of a challenge than she expected. Emily's neurotic parents are in the middle of a divorce and have no time to acknowledge their child's pain and grief. As a result, Emily tries to control the situation by not eating and exercising to exhaustion. Sarah gains strength as she tries to bring attention to Emily's needs.

Gottlieb, Lori. *Stick Figure: A Diary of My Former Self.* **New York: Simon & Schuster. 2000.**
Girls as young as 10 and 11 years of age are developing eating disorders as a way to control their weight as they enter puberty. *Stick Figure* is 11-year-old Lori's diary that she kept during 1978 as her weight plummeted below 60 pounds, and she was hospitalized for treatment. Lori recounts her life of wealth in which the message about looking good was constantly communicated. Lori tells us that all the girls at her school dieted and she often designed diets for them so they could lose weight. The only difference between Lori and the other girls is that she took her dieting more seriously and lost more weight. This book shows just how important it is to children to look sexy and appeal to boys.

Newman, Lesléa. *Fat Chance.* **New York: The Putnam & Grosset Group. 1994.**
Judi Liebowitz is an eighth grader who is convinced that she is overweight. Because Judi is hurt by the cruel comments her classmates make about her being plump, she decides to do something about this situation. Judi feels fortunate when Nancy Pratt shares her dieting secrets with her and shows her how to vomit after she's eaten. More than anything, Judi wants to look like the very thin Nancy, an aspiring model. Even though Judi's mother is disturbed that her daughter is trying to lose weight, she confuses the situation by forcing her to eat. This book has a strong message about the dangers of bingeing and purging.

Eating Disorders and Body Image Books for High School Readers

Burnett, Cheryl. *Life in the Fat Lane.* **New York: Bantam Doubleday Dell Books for Young Readers. 1998.**
Lara has led a charmed life. As a junior, she is voted homecoming queen and is following in the footsteps of her very attractive and image-conscious parents. When Lara starts gaining weight, she goes on a starvation diet and exercises nonstop because she would rather be "dead than fat." No matter how little Lara eats, she continues to gain weight, which her parents blame this on Lara's lack of discipline. As she gains weight, she loses friends. Eventually her boyfriend dumps her, too. It doesn't help that in the middle of her weight gain her parents move to Detroit to try to save their marriage. At this new high school, Lara is only known as a fat girl—not a former beauty pageant winner and homecoming queen. Eventually Lara comes to terms with her weight—but not without a struggle—and makes friends who are not hung up on thinness.

Corrigan, Eireann. *You Remind Me of You: A Poetry Memoir.* **New York: Scholastic. 2002.**
This book is a true-life account of a teen who spent her high school years battling eating disorders. Told in the form of poetry, this is the author's story about her eating disorder, the treatment she undergoes, and the boyfriend who stood by her side.

Hanauer, Cathi. *My Sister's Bones.* **New York: Dell Publishing Group. 1996.**
Told by Billie, a ninth grader, this book is about how her sister's anxiety and anorexia impact her. Cassie, a college freshman, is under considerable pressure by her heart surgeon father to get good grades. By Thanksgiving break, it is clear that she is also depressed, reclusive, and anorexic. Initially, Cassie's parents deny that there is a problem, but eventually they seek out medical support and place her in a hospital for treatment. Anorexia is one of the most difficult mental illnesses to treat, and after reading this book readers will have a better sense of why this is so. In addition to Cassie's anorexia, the book is interspersed with Billie's story about her first romance, her best friend's family which flees because they are wanted by the mob, and her first sexual experience.

Hautzig, Deborah. *Second Star to the Right.* **New York: Puffin Books. 1981.**
Based on the author's own experiences with anorexia, this story is about the bright, articulate, and talented Leslie Hiller. Even though she seems perfect to others, all she can see is fat. After losing a few pounds during a bout with the flu, she decides to continue losing weight by dieting. This realistic book tells the story of how Leslie is able to fool everyone into thinking that she is eating and the physical and mental problems she encounters during the illness. Eventually Leslie is hospitalized for treatment and begins to learn why she uses food to control her world. In the 1999 re-release of this book, the author writes an afterword

about her own experiences with anorexia and how she was finally able to combat the disease.

Hornbacher, Marya. *Wasted: A Memoir of Anorexia and Bulimia.* **New York: HarperCollins Publishers. 1998.**
Hornbacher's book is a memoir of her experience with anorexia and what she has learned from years of counseling. The addition of factual information about eating disorders is a bonus that frequently causes the book to read like an interesting psychology text. Anorexia is the most difficult psychological disorder to treat, and it is extremely important that teens who exhibit any of the characteristics of this disease receive immediate treatment. After completing Marya's story, the reader will have a much better understanding of the disease and just how easily it can take over a young life.

McNicoll, Sylvia. *Walking a Thin Line.* **New York: Scholastic. 1997.**
This book is unusual because of its message about media pressure that causes teens to do extraordinary things to be thin. Lauren wants to be perfect. As she sees it, losing 20 pounds is the way to achieve perfection. She begins a diet only after Andrea, the fattest girl in class, begins one and starts to lose weight. If Lauren does not lose weight, then she will be the fattest girl in the class and the butt of mean jokes. This is a solid book for teaching the facts about eating disorders, metabolism, and the food requirements of different body types. The story includes a doctor who patiently explains to Lauren that teens might put on a bit of weight just before they begin a growth spurt.

Sparks, Beatrice. *Kim: Empty Inside: The Diary of an Anonymous Teenager.* **New York: Avon Books. 2002.**
Kim thinks that if she could lose a few pounds, then her life would be perfect. During Kim's senior year at high school, she starts to diet so that everything will be perfect when she begins college in the fall and joins the gymnastic team. Kim's insecurities and desire for the perfect life lead her to engage in cycles of starvation, bingeing, and purging. The book contains some interesting factual information about the reasons for anorexia and the dangers of purging such as burst blood vessels in the eyes, tooth decay, and loss of tooth enamel.

Chapter Eight

Self-Inflicted Violence

Often called the addiction of the '90s, approximately two million people each year use self-inflicted physical injury as a means of coping with overwhelming psychological situations or feelings (Holmes 9). This behavior typically begins in adolescence, peaks in the mid-twenties and may disappear in the thirties. Without treatment, some self-injurers may continue well into their adult years. The reasons for self-injury are complex but are most often associated with histories of trauma such as physical and sexual abuse and parental neglect (Gallagher 639). Some teen girls who feel they have failed to live up to the idealized images portrayed in the media may develop an eating disorder or engage in self-harm as a form of self-punishment (AAMFT, par. 1).

> "She dropped the scissors into her lap, leaned against the wall of the locker room, and closed her eyes. The tensions of the morning seemed to drain away—all her doubts and fears were gone. She was completely relaxed now. The pain did that—it was like medicine, at least when it was used properly, it was."—
> *The Luckiest Girl in the World* by Steven Levenkron

Defined as the "deliberate attempt to harm or damage oneself without suicidal intent," self-injury is not suicide, but it is often mistaken as a suicidal act, even though the purposes are very different (Gallagher 638). The purpose of self-injury is to cope with the pressures of staying alive. The purpose of suicide is to end life (Alderman 103). Self-injury is intentional injury that is done to oneself on purpose without help from another person. While self-injury is horrifying to many people, it is a way to deal with emotional pain and trauma in the absence of more effective ways to communicate and cope (31). Adolescents who self-injure may feel powerless, alienated, and afraid. They have difficulty trusting others with their emotions. They feel that they are not good enough. In addition, these teens may be impulsive, depressed, and unable to plan for the future (Gallagher 640). They are sensitive to abandonment and rejection because their "sense of themselves and the ability to control their lives has been dictated so much by external events that they believe that their very existence depends on how others perceive them" (Strong 55).

"Miserable" is how many self-injurers would describe their childhoods (Strong 26). Two psychiatrists, Harold Graff and Richard Mallin, studied the characteristics common to cutters at a Philadelphia psychiatric hospital. They found that these cutters were young, highly intelligent women who were prone to alcohol and drug abuse and had great difficulty in relationships. They found that most of these self-injurers had experienced painful childhoods; their mothers were cold and rejecting; their fathers were distant and hypercritical (Strong 32). There is some debate about the gender that is most likely to commit self-injurious acts. Some mental health experts believe that self-injury is more prevalent in women (9) while others believe that the proportion of men to women is about equal (Alderman 19). Either way, self-injury is not just a problem of suburban teenage girls; it spans all cultural and socioeconomic groups (Strong 19).

Self-injurers may have a history of alcohol and drug abuse. This should not be surprising since the goals of both self-inflicted violence and using alcohol and drugs are the same: to change the mood or physical state of the abuser. However, self-injurers will rarely be under the influence of drugs or alcohol when they self-injure (Alderman 20). Other characteristics of self-injurers are: a history of parental alcohol and drug abuse, parental depression, family conflict and violence, eating disorders such as anorexia or bulimia, an inability to regulate emotions, a loss or disruption of an important or interpersonal relationship, and physical, sexual, or emotional abuse (Gallagher 629). Tracy Alderman, author of the self-help guide *The Scarred Soul*, writes that if "you engage in self-inflicted violence, chances are pretty good that you were abused as a child" (21). Not all self-injurers have been the victims of physical or sexual abuse; some self-injurers may have been verbally abused and demeaned. Some may have had to endure their parents' bitter divorce, their parents may have been too wrapped up in their own problems to recognize their children's needs, or they were pushed to live up to impossible standards of perfection (Gallagher 630). However, not every child who is abused will go on to become a self-injurer.

There are three types of self-injury. The first type, major self-injury, is very rare and includes self-castration and self-amputation. The second type is most often seen in people with autism, schizophrenia, and Tourette's syndrome. This type is called stereotypic self-injury and includes head banging, eyeball pressing, and arm biting. The most common form of self-injury, called superficial or moderate, involves cutting, burning, and skin picking (Ng 15). Other terms synonymous with self-injury are self-inflicted violence, self-mutilation, deliberate self-harm, self-destructive behavior, or "si." People who cut are called "cutters."

Princess Diana was a self-injurer. In her biography, Andrew Morton writes: "On one occasion she threw herself against a glass cabinet at Kensington Palace while on another she slashed at her wrists with a razor blade. Another time she cut herself with the serrated edge of a lemon slicer; on yet another occasion during a heated argument with Prince Charles, she picked up a penknife lying on his dressing table and cut her chest and thighs. Although she was bleeding, her husband scorned her. As ever, he thought she was faking her problems" (133). Another self-injurer, the actress and comedian Roseanne, says "she was unable to stop herself from clawing and gouging at all her "unseen" parts—breasts, belly, buttocks, thighs, genitals—after recovering memories of childhood physical and sexual abuse" (Strong 58).

The most prevalent form of self-injury is cutting. Most often cutting is done with a razor-blade, knife, piece of glass, or some other sharp object. Cuts are usually made on the arms, legs, wrists, or chest. However, self-injurers also cut themselves on other parts of their bodies that are hidden from view. Burning is another common form of self-injury in which individuals burn themselves with cigarettes, matches, lighters, kitchen-stove burners, or heated and burning objects. As with cuts, burns are usually made on the arms, legs, wrists, or chest. Other less common forms of self-injury are picking on wounds and scabs so they will not heal, hitting and bruising, severe nail biting, excessive scratching, breaking bones, and trichotillimania, or hair pulling, which results in the loss of hair from scalp, eyebrows, or beard (Alderman 25; AAMFT, par. 4).

Bridget, a patient described in Alderman's book, is a 19-year-old college student enrolled in honor-level courses who has many friends. She started burning herself when she was 14, stopped for a while and then resumed. Even though she lived in the college dorm, she still found the privacy to self-injure while others were asleep. When people notice her scars she tells them that they are a result of a childhood accident. Before she self-injures, Bridget is overwhelmed by negative feelings such as no one likes me, I hate my body, nothing ever works out right, no one would ever want to be with me, I'm so stupid, life sucks, I hate everyone, I can't stand my life, and I want someone to care about me (71). Other teens may experience similar emotions such as frustration and anger, alienation, and depression before they self-injure. Because self-injurers are unable to verbally communicate their inner pain, their injuries are a way to express it and take control. The actual self-injury often occurs in a trance-like state called dissociation in which self-injurers report that they do not feel pain and may not even be aware of what they are doing. Because the individual feels depersonalized, numb, and unreal, the self-injury is used to snap them back into consciousness (Strong 38).

For some, the self-injury produces chemicals, called endorphins, which help them feel calmer, happier, and more peaceful (Alderman 8). "For cutters, it is a strangely effective coping method for dealing with an inner pain so overwhelming it must be brought to the surface. If they are comforted by pain, it is generally because it is all they have ever known" (Strong xviii). Because self-inflicted violence is so effective in reducing tension and establishing a temporary feeling of well-being, self-injurers may have a hard time quitting the behavior. Self-injury serves to distract from, not alleviate, the pain (43). As long as self-injurers do not learn other methods for coping with negative emotions, the cycle will continue as tension builds and self-injury is once again used to soothe the pain (Alderman 78).

The actual act of self-injury tends to follow a certain ritualistic pattern: a specific location in the home; the use of particular types of instruments, preparation of the instruments and the environment; and dressing the wounds after the self-injury. Self-injurers will often have a favorite room in their homes, such as a bathroom, a bedroom, or even a closet, where the self-mutilation will occur. Self-injurers tend to have favorite instruments, such as razors, knives, or matches, and will not use other objects even if they are readily available and could produce similar injuries. Also, self-injurers may prepare their space, by lighting candles, drawing bath water, and laying out the instruments. Afterwards, they may bandage their wounds a particular way, take a hot bath, or write about the incident in their journals (Alderman 62).

After the self-inflicted injury, individuals report that the tension felt before the self-injury has lessened. However, once the relief has worn off, the negative emotions can return (Alderman 75). Because self-inflicted violence is so misunderstood, self-injurers may feel shame and embarrassment and want to hide their injuries from friends and family members by wearing long-sleeve shirts and long pants even in hot weather. They may also make excuses for their scars. For instance, self-injurers might blame the injury on a cat, a work-related injury, or, as in Bridget's case, a childhood accident.

Alderman recommends that people support self-injurers by not showing horror or negativity toward their wounds and by recognizing the high amount of emotional distress that they feel (180). Self-injurers should be encouraged to receive psychological treatment so that the root problem or trauma can be addressed. Treatment for self-injury usually consists of individual and group therapy to change the behavior and drug-related treatments to control the condition. Treatment can take place at community mental health centers, local clinics, hospitals, and in other specialized programs (Gallagher 640; Holmes 48). The American Association for Marriage and Family Therapy recommends family therapy as the most effective treatment for adolescent self-injury problems. They also recommend skill-building groups that can help self-injurers learn new ways of coping with stress and pain, learn effective tools for managing their moods and challenging unhelpful thinking, adopt visualization and meditation skills, and adopt healthy methods to better manage stress (AAMFT, par. 6–7).

Self-Inflicted Violence Books for Middle School Readers

Levenkron, Steven. *The Luckiest Girl in the World*. New York: Penguin Books. 1997.
If you only purchase one fiction book about self-injury, this is the one to buy. The author, a psychotherapist, has written a believable and attractive story about 15-year-old Katie Roskova, a competitive ice-skater, who self-injures. Katie's mother is very demanding and keeps pushing her to skate, even as Katie is obviously struggling and wants to quit. Because of her mother's venomous and aggressive behavior, Katie is unable to stand up for herself. She begins to cut whenever pressures to be perfect become too much. Readers will develop an understanding about the dynamics of individual and group therapies that are used to help a self-injurer deal with the original trauma. As Katie learns to communicate, she is able to stop cutting. Many teens will be able to relate to the demands and pressures to be perfect, the absent father, and the domineering, mean-spirited mother. This book will make an excellent addition to a secondary school fiction collection and is good supplementary reading for students in a health or psychology class who want to learn more about stress and effective coping skills.

Self-Inflicted Violence Books for High School Readers

Goobie, Beth. *The Dream Where the Losers Go.* **Montreal: Roussan Publishers Inc. 1999.**

This is a disturbing book about Skey, a cutter, who has spent the past five months living in a treatment facility. In much of the book, she experiences disassociation because she is unable to deal with trauma. In her English class, she makes friends with a boy who was sexually abused. They are able to help each other realize that they do not need to hide in the "tunnels" of their minds anymore. Teens who self-harm often have a history of abuse, sometimes sexual, and control by others. They are not able to find their voices and stand up for themselves. In this story, Skey has lived with an abusive father, dated a controlling boyfriend, and been gang raped. The story ends on a happy note as Skey is finally able to communicate in words what happened to her and has made two friends who help her regain her spirit.

Kettlewell, Caroline. *Skin Game: A Memoir.* **New York: St. Martin's Press. 1999.**

Skin Game is a true-life account of Caroline's 20 years in which she cuts as a way to cope with anxiety and depression. She was never abused, but her family's dynamics caused her to become very self-conscious and alienated. Because this story is written when the author is an adult and reflects back on the years that she cut, this book may be more than a teen wants to read. It is only recommended for the most sophisticated high school students. Two chapters — 11 and 12 — are extraordinarily insightful and are must reads for anyone who wants to understand why teens cut and the situations that cause them to vent their frustrations via the razor.

McCormick, Patricia. *Cut.* **New York: Asheville, NC: Front Street. 2000.**

The first time Callie cut herself was at home. It was with an Exacto knife. Callie remembers what it felt like when she "placed the blade next to the skin on my palm" and how the "floor tipped up at me and my body spiraled away" (3). But what she really remembers is the relief. Callie tells her story as a "guest" from Sea Pines. Also known as "Sick Minds," there are guests with food issues, guests with substance-abuse issues, and guests, like Callie, with behavioral issues. This book will help teens learn about treatment in a hospital environment. For much of the book, Callie is unable to speak, but we read her thoughts on the pages of this book. Eventually, gentle counseling coaxes Callie to realize that cutting is not the problem, only its manifestation. In Callie's case, a disorganized family, uncommunicative parents, and her own guilt over her sick brother's near death are what spark her cutting.

Wilson, Dawn. *Saint Jude.* **Greensboro, NC: Tudor Publishers. 2001.**

Taylor has been deposited at the Saint Jude Hospital's Outpatient Program to receive counseling and treatment for her manic depressive state. In this outpatient home where she lives, she meets other teens who are dealing with a variety of mental illnesses such as depression and schizophrenia. With the help of her guitar and some lucky breaks, Taylor is one of the only teens in this story who heals enough to lead a normal life. *Saint Jude* is categorized with other self-harm books because Taylor cuts and harms herself when things become too much for her to handle. This book provides readers with a glimpse into hospital life for upper-middle class teens who have the financial resources to receive this level of treatment. At the beginning of each chapter, there is a sentence from the Saint Jude's orientation booklet. Chapter 31 states that "Mental illness is very common, although few are willing to talk about it."

Wittlinger, Ellen. "Stevie in the Mirror." *On the Edge: Stories at the Brink.* **Ed. Lois Duncan. New York: Simon & Schuster Books for Young Readers. 2000.** Suicide attempt or self-injury? You decide. Whichever, Stevie is depressed over her father's death and her mother's remarriage. Now her mother is going to have a baby, and Stevie is feeling insignificant and invalidated. After Stevie cuts herself, she is immediately sent to a psychiatric hospital for treatment. She soon learns that she doesn't belong at the hospital with the other patients who have much more significant problems than hers. Stevie's roommate has had a nervous breakdown and cannot talk, but she nevertheless advises her: Do not forget to cry. This short story is appropriate for a teen who is feeling replaced by a new half-sibling.

Chapter Nine

Divorce

With the divorce rate hovering at about 50%, it is certain that librarians, media specialists, and other youth workers will come in contact with teens who have been affected by divorce. More than 75% of the divorced parents will remarry. Because the rate of divorce is higher for second marriages, many teens may experience additional stress when that marriage unravels. Mental health researchers and practitioners disagree about the negative consequences of divorce because each breakup is unique. Some say that even though divorce increases a child's risk for a variety of problems, not all children will be affected similarly. Many factors influence the outcome of the divorce. Some of these factors are the age of the child when the divorce occurs, the temperament of the child, the parent's competency and ability to parent, the amount of conflict prior to and after the divorce, and whether the divorce will substantially lower the teen's standard of living (*Divorce and Its Impact on Teens*, par. 7).

> "It's been 63 64 days since the Divorce. Mom says we have to move forward and that every day things will get a little easier. Nothing is one bit easier. Dad says Sam and I have to be tough. Maybe I'd be tougher if my stomach didn't hurt half the time" —
> *The Top-Secret Journal of Fiona Claire Jardin* by Robin Cruise

The age of the child is important because divorce is internalized depending on the child's stage of development. Preschool children are more likely to focus on maintaining emotional security and relationships with both parents. Middle school-age children may assume guilt, blame, or responsibility for their parent's divorce. Teens are more likely to deal with divorce cognitively. They wonder how the divorce will affect them (Miller, Ryan, and Morrison 286).

One of the consequences of divorce is loss of income, which may lead to lowered standard of living, welfare, residential changes, maternal employment, and poverty (Haggerty et al. 67). Teens will most likely be concerned about the disruption to their own plans and "they suspect the divorce may have direct financial ramifications for them, and they're usually right" (*Adolescents and Divorce*, par. 3). Because money is tight, teens may need to work. According to researchers, even though part-time jobs may increase self-esteem and provide additional income, adolescents who work more than half-time report higher levels of emotional distress, substance abuse, and engage in first intercourse at an earlier age (Blum 33).

In a longitudinal study of 131 children of divorce, Wallerstein, Lewis, and Blakeslee compared these children's financial support for college with teens from intact families. They found that fewer than 30% of teens from divorced families received full or consistently partial support for college. However, 90% of teens from intact families received full or consistently partial support for college. They blame the discrepancy on the fact that a greater proportion of the salary of divorced parents may be required for living expenses. Some parents who have remarried and started another family may be unwilling or unable to pay college expenses for a child from a previous marriage or one who is not biologically related. The financial aid forms require that teens' custodians (most likely the biological mother and stepfather) report both incomes even when one is unwilling or unable to pay for college. When financial needs are calculated using both incomes, children of divorce may not be eligible for loans and need-based scholarships because their family's income exceeds the salary threshold. As a result, children of divorce may end up less well-educated than their peers from intact families even when the parents are college educated. This inability to receive college scholarships has long-term economic and social consequences on teens of divorce (249).

Other than income loss, the change in family life that has been most clearly documented to be a negative consequence of divorce is children's loss of contact with their nonresidential parents. "Data from a nationally representative sample of a recent cohort of divorces indicates that, on average, nonresidential parents see their children very infrequently. The most optimistic estimate indicates that following divorce approximately one-third of children see their fathers a couple of times a year or less, while only a quarter see them weekly or more" (Haggerty et al. 69).

The initial stages of the divorce are the most traumatic. It is during this time that there could be a partial or complete collapse of an adult's ability to parent. Many parents may be caught up in rebuilding their own lives. Sometimes one child in the family, usually the oldest, assumes responsibility for nurturing the younger children. The oldest children may become the "parent for their own parents during the years that follow" (Wallerstein, Lewis, and Blakeslee xiv). Teens who take on too much responsibility can negatively impact their academic studies, school friendships and activities, and their sense of being a child (8).

Conflict is another factor that can be detrimental to teens. Parents who divorce are more likely than those who maintain their marriages to have experienced pre-break-up difficulties. Some arguments may focus on alcoholism, drug abuse, physical and emotional abuse, disagreements about gender roles, and other incompatibilities. Over time, children who live in homes where there is conflict and chaos, whether a divorce occurs or not, will show more deleterious affects (Rodriguez and Arnold, pars. 8, 11). No matter the age the divorce occurs, prior to the divorce most children will show behavioral problems.

Divorce should be viewed as a transition rather than a one-time event. Children may begin to feel the negative effects of the divorce up to one year before the actual separation. Divorce can mean a decrease in financial status because proportionally more of the income is required to pay living expenses. Teens may be negatively impacted when a stay-at-home parent returns to work. An increase in parental work hours means the parent may be less available to drive the teen to sports practice, monitor homework, or attend school functions (Adolescence, par. 1). Researchers believe that many of the problems children encounter from divorce are the result of financial hardship and poverty as a result of the loss of one income. This reduction in family economic resources and standard of living is partly associated with disruptive and antisocial behavior, especially in boys.

Children who are intelligent, socially mature, responsible, and have easy dispositions are most likely to adjust to divorce with the fewest problems (*Adolescence*, pars. 2–3). Teen boys and girls tend to react differently to divorce. Teen boys' difficulties more often occur just after the divorce. After divorce, boys' self-esteem declines more than girls'. "Boys from divorced families displayed poorer performance than intact-family males on mental health measures, evidenced higher frequencies of dependency, irrelevant talk, withdrawal, blaming, and inattention as well as decreased work effort and higher frequencies of inappropriate behavior, unhappiness, and maladaptive symptoms" (Rodriguez and Arnold, par. 41). Immediately following divorce, teen boys report an increase in substance abuse which is greater than that of boys with continuously married parents. In addition, marital disruption lowers boys' mathematics and reading performances. However, researchers believe that this may be offset when the breakup means the termination of a high-conflict relationship (par. 39).

Many of the teen girls' difficulties occur prior to the marital separation. In addition, teen girls may become involved in early sexual behavior which could lead to a greater risk of teenage pregnancy. Teen girls tend to be at risk of the "sleeper effect," which typically affects them in late adolescence or early adulthood when the psychosocial crisis of intimacy is being resolved. The "sleeper effect" is a high level of anxiety and fear of betrayal in romantic relationships. When older teen girls experience the "sleeper effect," they are connecting anxious feelings about their parents' divorce with anxiety about their own relationships. Teen males do not experience the "sleeper effect." Marital disruption is not associated with declines in socially acceptable behavior for teen girls, but it is for boys (Rodriguez and Arnold, pars. 37, 38).

As a result of divorce, teens may experience depression. School performance may suffer as a result of truancy and opposition to authority. They may abuse drugs. Teens may be unable to cope with daily activities and show marked changes in sleeping or eating habits. Some teens may complain of physical ailments such as headaches or stomachaches. Other teens may try to control the situation by becoming anorexic.

Because divorce can negatively impact educational outcomes, educators should be aware of the consequences of divorce. Teachers should not interpret declining academic performance as lack of interest (Miller, Ryan, and Morrison 286). They must attempt to buffer, or minimize, these effects.

Researchers believe that promoting resiliency is important because children of divorce may "bear an unprecedented responsibility for raising themselves" (Wallerstein, Lewis, and Blakeslee 265). The resiliency factors of mentorship, a warm and caring school environment, involvement in activities or with sports, and development of their own strengths, interests, and talents could be helpful (299). Other ways educators can foster resiliency is by building skills in goal setting, visioning, drug prevention, and gang resistance. Teachers can also promote to students volunteer activities that will enable them to care for their community and their neighbors. Organized mentoring relationships by caring adults can be as simple as having lunch with a child once a month (Wong 6).

The family can be supported through parenting classes and by planning parent and teacher conferences to focus on ways to help the student succeed. What matters to teens is "time and attention, lots of love, peace and consistency between parents, and freedom from poverty" (*Adolescence*, par. 2).

Divorce Books for Middle School Readers

Cruise, Robin. *The Top-Secret Journal of Fiona Claire Jardin*. New York: Harcourt. 1998.
Fiona's parents have recently divorced and she is feeling much confusion and pain. Besides not having her father around every day, the biggest loss is moving from her spacious home into a smaller and more affordable apartment. She also finds that living part of the week with one parent or the other is very disorienting. Fiona cannot remember if she left her favorite clothes at her mother's or her father's. Because Fiona refuses to cry about the divorce, her therapist thinks she is in denial and suggests that she keep a journal. After the first year of the divorce, Fiona rereads passages from her diary and realizes how much she and her younger brother have gone through—from shell-shock to acceptance—and how time has begun to heal their emotional pain. She comes to understand that even though the family structure is different, they are nonetheless still a family. This warm and uplifting book is highly recommended for students who are struggling with their parent's divorce.

High, Linda Oatman. *The Summer of the Great Divide*. New York: Holiday House. 1996.
Wheezie is shipped off to her aunt and uncle's for the summer so that her parents can work out their separation. Besides hating the idea that her parents are divorcing—she says that having her heart cut in two could not be any more painful—she hates the idea of having to spend the summer on a farm where they pick vegetables and slaughter animals. Wheezie decides to get even with her parents by running away with her annoying cousin, a special education student, but it does not stop the divorce.

Hobbs, Valerie. *Charlie's Run*. New York: Farrar, Straus and Giroux. 2000.
When Charlie's parents tell him that they are divorcing, he devises a scheme to get them back together by running away from home. As he is leaving town, he stops at the local donut shop where he is picked up by Doo, an unusual girl who is driving a yellow Volkswagen beetle and who is heading to Los Angeles to escape her stepfather's abuse. Along the way Charlie and Doo learn a lot about divorce and families. There is a strong anti-drug message in this book. Charlie's Boy Scout and CPR skills help save the life of a drug pusher who overdoses. Even though Charlie wants to get his parents back together, he realizes that the divorce is not about him.

Koss, Amy Goldman. *Stranger in Dadland*. New York: Dial Books. 2001.
Every summer 12-year-old John flies from Kansas to visit his father in Los Angeles. Each summer he keeps hoping that he and his father will spend quality

time together doing fun activities, but this never happens. This summer will even be worse than the previous ones because his sister refuses to leave Kansas and his father has a girlfriend, Cora, who is demanding all his time. John is especially upset when he realizes that his father's new friends have no idea he exists. After John's father drags him to business meetings, he decides to fight back.

Mack, Tracy. *Drawing Lessons*. New York: Scholastic Press. 2000.
Drawing Lessons is a physically beautiful book about Aurora, a talented middle schooler, whose parents separate after she witnesses her artist father kissing one of his models and she tells. Aurora has always had a close relationship with her father based on their mutual love of art, but now she closes her heart to painting and drawing. After confronting her father about her pain and anger, Aurora slowly returns to painting with new strength. Although the characters in this book are middle school-aged, this elegant story will be embraced by high school students who are facing their parent's divorce.

Robinson, Lee. *Gateway*. Boston: Houghton Mifflin Company. 1996.
Teens who are sick and tired of being shuttled back and forth between warring parents will certainly relate to this story. When 13-year-old Margaret Whitford starts having trouble remembering whether she is supposed to be spending the night at her mother's or father's, she decides to fight back. The court appoints an eccentric older woman as guardian ad litem who hires a lawyer to ensure Margaret's right to live in her own home. As a result, Margaret stays in the house full-time and her parents move in and out, alternating on a schedule arranged by the court. This is called nesting.

Rodowsky, Colby. *Spindrift*. New York: Farrar, Straus and Giroux. 2000.
During the summer between seventh and eighth grades, Cassie's life goes through more turmoil than she could ever anticipate. She had expected that the biggest event would be the birth of her older sister's first baby. However, when Cassie sees her brother-in-law, Mickey, snuggling with another woman at a party, she knows things will never be the same. Divorce affects the entire family, and Cassie is devastated when she finds that Mickey, whom she idolized, would do such a thing. This story will help younger siblings cope with the divorce of an older sister or brother.

Shalant, Phyllis. *The Great Eye*. New York: Puffin Books. 1996.
Lucy Rising, who is going into eighth grade, is looking forward to spending a relaxing summer with her sister, Anna, a college sophomore. Lucy hopes that Anna can help her deal with her parent's separation and her father's move to Australia to be with another woman. But Anna has a boyfriend now and wants to spend all her free time with him. What saves Lucy is Hobart, a beautiful dog that she is training to become a seeing-eye guide. As it turns out, Hobart has been hurt, too, and needs his self-confidence restored. This is a comforting book for middle school students who are going through the beginning stages of a divorce and are wondering how they will ever cope with these changes and adjustments.

Siebold, Jan. *Rope Burn.* **Morton Grove, IL: Albert Whitman & Company. 1998.**
Although Richard has always enjoyed writing, he is failing at it. Once writing is called an "assignment," his mind goes blank. However, Richard finds an ingenious way to combine a writing assignment with his knowledge about divorce. The assignment is to select a proverb that illustrates an event that has happened in his life. In this book, Richard writes about divorce from the perspective of eight proverbs such as "One good turn deserves another," "He who hesitates is lost," and "If at first you don't succeed, try, try again."

Warner, Sally. *Sister Split.* **Middleton, WI: Pleasant Company Publications. 2001.**
When 11-year-old Ivy Miller's parents separate, she stays with her mother while her sister Lacey goes to live with her father in his rented apartment. After a weekend visit to her father's apartment, Ivy decides she has had enough of her sister's nasty comments, and they get into an all out fist fight. To force them to become friends again, their parents lock them together in a room for the weekend. *Sister Split* provides an interesting perspective on divorce and its effect on siblings who no longer live together.

Weeks, Sarah. *Guy Time.* **New York: HarperCollins Publishers. 2000.**
Thirteen-year-old Guy Strang's parents are getting a divorce. His father has moved across the country to California leaving Guy, who is just beginning to deal with his own developing interest in girls, to watch his middle-age mother turn into a man-crazed vixen. In desperation, Guy tries to reunite his parents by writing a love letter to his father on behalf of his mother and signs her name. Even though the letter does not reunite his parents, his father realizes Guy needs him. He leaves California to move near Guy.

Divorce Books for High School Readers

Caseley, Judith. *Losing Louisa.* **New York: Farrar, Straus and Giroux. 1999.**
While a teen pregnancy is central to this book, the overall issue is how a family changes as a result of infidelity, divorce, and remarriage. With great humor and insight, Lacey, the narrator of the story, recounts how her mother morphs almost overnight from a dowdy housewife to a crazed woman on the lookout for men. Teens who have witnessed this transformation will be able to relate to Lacey's feelings of confusion and discomfort. It does not help that her father remarries and has a new baby. Lacey and Rosie, her sister, are hurt to see how much better their father treats his new wife than he did their mother.

Cohn, Rachel. *Gingerbread.* **New York: Simon & Schuster Books for Young Readers. 2002.**
In this raucous story, Cyd Charisse is so out of control that her mother and stepfather ban her to her room—a place she calls "Alcatraz." When this move does not tame the wild Cyd, her mother, whom she calls "the lovely Nancy," sends her to spend a few weeks with her biological father. Nancy hopes that when Cyd gets to know her "bio" father, she will be cured of the longing to live with him.

During Cyd's stay, she meets her two half-siblings and learns that she is the product of a love relationship while her "bio" father was married. She also learns why her mother would have given her such a strange name.

Cooney, Caroline. *Tune In Anytime*. **New York: Delacorte Press. 1999.**

Although the plot in this book is extreme, this is a fun and crazy book that raises tough questions about love, commitment, and the first family. Sophie Olivette's father has just met and fallen in love with her sister's college roommate. In just a weekend, the two decide to marry. Sophie's father intends to sell their mansion-like home so that he and his new trophy wife can travel around the world. In a very short time, Sophie and her mother are evicted from their beautiful home and are deposited in a small apartment with a view of the dumpster. This book raises questions and concerns about a teen's financial uncertainty, a lowered standard of living, and being left behind for a new family. Sophie wants her family back because she says even a dysfunctional family is better than a divorced one. Teens will laugh from the first to the last page.

Dessen, Sarah. *That Summer*. **New York: Puffin Books. 1996.**

This is an easy-to-digest story about the double-whammy summer that the nearly six foot tall, 15-year-old Haven endures when her sportscaster father marries the "Weather Pet," the woman who broke up her parent's marriage, and her sister, Ashley, marries the boring Lewis. Haven cannot understand why her vivacious and daring sister could settle for the likes of Lewis. Teens who are dealing with their father's remarriage will relate to the emotions that Haven feels—guilt, distrust, and loss of family. Eventually Haven understands the appeal of Lewis to Ashley. In a very quiet way, Dessen communicates to teens that even though things do not always work out as intended, life goes on.

Dessen, Sarah. *This Lullaby*. **New York: Viking. 2002.**

Remy's mother is a serial divorcee who has been married four times. As a result, Remy has become a very good wedding, and divorce, planner. Even though Remy thinks her mother should stay single, her mother believes it is far worse not to take a chance on love. After all the marriages and divorces Remy has witnessed, her philosophy is to protect herself. She is notorious for dumping guys as soon as they get too close. That is until she meets Dexter whose own mother has been divorced six times. *This Lullaby* is a funny but warm story about a high school girl who is facing another one of her mother's divorces just as she is falling in love for the first time and preparing to leave for college.

Mackler, Carolyn. *Love and Other Four-Letter Words*. **New York: Dell Laurel-Leaf Books. 2000.**

Being in high school is tough enough, but when Sammie's parents break the news they are separating, her whole life spirals downward. Instead of spending a year in California while her father is on sabbatical from his college teaching position, she will be living in New York City. She is not pleased. To begin with, she cannot take her beloved bike. Second, she has to leave her best friend. Once she actually arrives in the "Big Apple," she finds the apartment is too small, she has no friends, and her mother is depressed and cries all the time. But Sammie takes charge and develops strengths that previously she could only have imagined. Sammie realizes that even though her life is different, she will survive.

Velásquez, Gloria. *Maya's Divided World.* **Houston, TX: Piñata Books. 1995.**
This book belongs to the Roosevelt High Series which features multiracial teens who are dealing with tough problems. In this book, Maya is devastated when her parents divorce. She blames her mother for the breakup. Maya believes that in their Hispanic culture, women are not to divorce. As a result of her anger, Maya joins a rough group of teens, her grades plummet, and she drops off the tennis team. It does not help that her father claims he is too busy to see her. With help from her friends and a counselor, Maya is able to deal with her anger. Although she realizes her life will never be the same, she stops being angry at her mother and establishes a regular schedule of visitation with her father.

Wyss, Thelma Hatch. *Ten Miles from Winnemucca.* **New York: HarperCollins Publishers. 2002.**
Ever since Martin J. Miller's father died when he was five years old, it has just been he and his mom, whom he calls "Mom Miller." For all these years, the two of them have been just fine. When Mom Miller, a teacher, returns from a summer certification course, she brings with her a boyfriend who soon turns into a fiancé. Within a short time, Martin and his mother have packed up and moved to Seattle to live with her fiancé and his son, Burgess, who resents the impending marriage as much as Martin does. Soon after the wedding, the newlyweds leave for a three month honeymoon to Europe and Burgess makes good on his anger by throwing all of Martin's belongings out the window. After Burgess pours beer on the heap, Martin takes the hint. He puts his soggy belongings in his Jeep and starts driving. He ends up in Red Rock, Idaho, where he spends three months living in the woods. Even though he is not pleased with his mom's new husband and feels betrayed, he realizes that his home is with her. In the book, Martin reminisces about life in a single-parent family and wonders what he missed by not growing up with a father. In an uplifting way, this book deals with the very real concerns teens face when parents remarry.

Chapter Ten

Teen Pregnancy

Teen age pregnancy is a major social, economic, and political issue that has severe consequences for both mother and child. According to the National Center for Health Statistics, almost one million girls under the age of 20 become pregnant every year. Approximately 29,000 are under the age of 14 (Pruitt 162). Although pregnancy rates decreased in the '90s, they are still higher than any other industrialized nation on earth (Nitz 525). About one-third of these teen pregnancies will be aborted, 4% of the live births will be released for adoption, and the rest of the children will be raised by their teen mothers. More teen mothers are opting to keep and raise their children while remaining unmarried. In the 1960s, 21% of teen mothers adopted out their babies. At that time only 15% of all teen mothers remained unmarried, but the percentage in 1992 rose to 72% (Kivisto 1045). One-third of these teen mothers will have a repeat pregnancy within two years after their first delivery (East and Felice 36).

> "My parents never talked much to me about getting pregnant or going 'too far.' I was the daughter they never worried about."—
> *Don't Think Twice*
> by Ruth Pennebaker

Even though the teen pregnancy rate is still high, factors responsible for the decrease in teen pregnancies are greater use of condoms, the adoption of effective injectable and implant contraceptives, and the leveling off of teen sexual activity (CDC, par. 2). Despite the fact that teen pregnancy rates for all racial and ethnic groups declined during the five years between 1991 to 1996, young women of color continue to have high rates. In 2000, birth rates per 1,000 women ages 15–17 were: 15.9 for White Non-Hispanic teens; 50.2 for African-American teens; and 60 for Hispanic teens (Martin, Hamilton, and Ventura 3). Pregnancy and birth rate figures among teenagers vary substantially from state to state. Some states have rates almost three times higher than states with the lowest rates.

Girls are more likely to become pregnant if they are poor, failing in school, have family problems, or their mothers were teenage parents. Tamara Kreinin, the director of state and local affairs for the National Campaign to Prevent Teen Pregnancy, says that "One of the biggest predictors of teen pregnancy is educational failure" ("Curricular Programs," 39). Teens may become pregnant when they do not have a reason not to (Kivisto 1058). Likewise, teen pregnancy contributes to educational failure. Teens who become pregnant are less likely to graduate from high school, get a good job, or go to college. Teen mothers are more likely to be poor, on welfare, and users of illegal drugs and alcohol (Curricular Programs 39). Researchers have found that resiliency characteristics impact teen pregnancy rates, too. For instance, adolescents who had a strong sense of control over their lives were less likely to experience teenage childbirth (Hanson, Myers, and Ginsburg 244). Teen mothers are more apt to be passive and let other people take charge of their lives (Kivisto 1058). Teens with a low sense of control increase the risk of second or third pregnancies (Lewis, Ross, and Mirowsky 1594). Self-esteem and self-efficacy were predictors of a teen's ability to say "No" to unwanted sex (Zimmerman et al. 396). Other researchers have found that teen mothers tend to have nebulous educational, career, and family goals when compared to their peers who had not become pregnant. Teens with strong connections to their schools are more likely to postpone sexual activity and other risky behaviors (Resnick, Bearman, and Blum 824).

In a study by Kivisto, teen mothers who were engaging in risky unprotected sex were compared to teen clients of a family practice clinic who were using birth control. He found that the high-risk teens differed from the teens using birth control in a number of ways. The high-risk teen mothers had lower family incomes, were less successful in school, and were less involved in extracurricular activities. The high-risk teens were more likely to engage in drinking, smoking, and drug use. The friends of the high-risk teens placed a lower value on school, were less involved in extracurricular activity, and were less inclined to be involved in voluntary and community organizations than the friends of teens who were not at risk of becoming pregnant. The friends of high-risk teens were more likely to be involved in gangs, to be in trouble with the police, and to be sexually active. He found that teen mothers "lacked sufficient incentives to prevent themselves from becoming pregnant" (Kivisto 1058). Even though African-American teens were only 15% of the survey, they represented 44% of the high-risk teen mothers. (1045).

The children of teen mothers suffer as well. These children are more at risk for behavior and school problems (Nitz 525). Sixty-six percent of children living with mothers who have never been married live below the poverty level. Poverty is associated with a variety of social problems. These include crime, substance abuse, welfare dependency, and low educational attainment. Because children born to teen mothers tend to live in less supportive households, they are more likely to do poorly in school, be abused and neglected, and have a greater likelihood of becoming pregnant when they reach their own teen years (Kivisto 1045). Kreinin says that 70% of the prisoners in the United States were children of teen mothers (Curricular programs 40).

Although early parenting is regarded by most adults as a mistake, some teens are happy about their pregnancies. Teens may see pregnancy as a way to turn their lives around. "Pregnancy and parenthood may appear to be positive options for teens living in poor communities with few positive roles models and no job opportunities" (Nitz 526). Davies, McKinnon, and Rains found the opinions of the people around the pregnant teen, particularly her boyfriend, family, and friends, to influence her feelings and decision about going through with the pregnancy and birth of the baby (91).

Although most teens have been exposed to sex education at school and know about birth control, they still have difficulty finding safe, easy, and satisfactory methods to use. One reason is the decision to use birth control must be constantly renewed as teen relationships begin, change, and end. Even when teens have become sexually active, only about one-third said they had sex in the past three months. Because many teens have sex infrequently, they do not stay on a consistent and constant form of birth control. They may change from method to method depending on the relationship. It is at the beginning of the relationship before birth control options have been discussed that most teen pregnancies occur (Kivisto 1045).

"Every 26 seconds, another adolescent gets pregnant," says Gerald Tirozzi, who was the assistant secretary for elementary and secondary education at the U.S. Department of Education. Between 1985 and 1990, the cost of teen pregnancy was $120 billion. "We need to remind our leaders of the cost of not funding [prevention] programs" ("Curricular Programs," 30). As a result of the widespread concern about teen pregnancy, many intervention programs have been established. These interventions include pregnancy prevention education, providing access to contraception, and community-based programs offering a broad variety of educational and job skills as alternatives to pregnancy. The programs use a variety of approaches, including hospital- or clinic-based, school-based, and home visitation services (Nitz 526). Effective teen programs communicate a clear message that "adolescence is a time for education and growing up. Teen pregnancy is not okay" ("Curricular Programs," 41). Effective programs contain the following elements:

- They are age appropriate and sensitive to the culture of the program participants;
- They are of sufficient duration for teens to acquire appropriate skills to prevent pregnancy;
- They utilize various teaching styles and methods to communicate the message about pregnancy;
- They provide practice with regard to peer communication and assertiveness training;
- They focus on issues such as education and job training; and
- They include males and other family members in the interventions (Nitz 530).

Schools can help reduce teen pregnancy by offering programs that go beyond didactic sex education. Effective programs build resiliency by promoting educational success, by developing skills that help build a positive future and a strong sense of purpose, and teaching teens to say "No" (National Campaign to Prevent Teen Pregnancy 1).

Teen Pregnancy Books for Middle School Readers

Ferris, Amy Schor. *A Greater Goode*. Boston: Houghton Mifflin Company. 2002.
    In addition to teen pregnancy, the characters in *A Greater Goode* are also dealing with divorce, abuse, giftedness, and running away. In this story, Addie Goode

observes a young pregnant woman at K-Mart being verbally abused by her boyfriend. When Addie learns that this woman, Rachel, is living in the woods in an old abandoned church, she invites Rachel to stay in her family's garage and gives her food and clothing. Listening to Rachel's problems causes Addie to relive the confusion and hurt she still feels since her mother ran off and abandoned the family. Because Addie cannot deal with these emotions, she asks Rachel to leave. In a twist of fate, Addie is able to reunite Rachel with her mother who is in the terminal stages of cancer.

Fine, Anne. *Flour Babies*. Boston: Bantam Doubleday Books for Young Readers. 1992.
The underachieving boys in Room 8 at the St. Boniface School need to select a science fair project. The one they chose is the "The Great Flour Baby Experiment." For three weeks, each boy in Room 8 is required to carry around a six-pound sack of flour. They pretend the sack is a baby who must be nurtured and kept from harm. Most of the boys do not take this experiment seriously; however, Simon Martin, a physically large but previously irresponsible boy, bonds with his sack of flour. This parenting experience allows Simon to come to terms with his father's desertion. He is able to identify the traits that make a good father.

Oughton, Jerrie. *Perfect Family*. Boston: Houghton Mifflin Company. 2000.
The setting for this book is the coastal lowlands of North Carolina in the 1950s. Fifteen-year-old Welcome Marie O'Neal falls in love with Nicholas Canton, a North Carolina State football player extraordinaire. At an early fall square dance, Nicholas gets drunk and tries to rape Welcome. She fights him off, but his actions end their relationship. Because she cannot stop thinking about him, she tries to replace him by having sex with a high school friend. When she announces to her parents that she is pregnant, they put her on a bus to await the baby's birth at the home of her aunt and uncle, a childless couple, in Virginia Beach. Welcome becomes an avid library user as she searches for books about the baby's prenatal development. Even though Welcome wants to keep the baby, she realizes a child needs two parents.

Teen Pregnancy Books for High School Readers

Bechard, Margaret. *Hanging on to Max*. Brookfield, CT: Roaring Brook Press. 2002.
Most teen pregnancy books are written from the perspective of the mother, but *Hanging on to Max* is told by Sam Pettigrew, a high school senior, who has a baby son, Max. After Sam's girlfriend becomes pregnant, she decides to put the baby up for adoption. When Sam learns about this decision, he fights to gain custody because he wants to raise Max. Instead of playing football, going to parties, and making college plans, Sam attends a special school for pregnant teens and takes care of Max. Without support from his father, Sam is constantly tired and misses the normal teen antics with his friends. Gradually Sam realizes that

he is a child himself and is not prepared to care for Max. He reluctantly gives Max up for adoption. *Hanging on to Max* provides a glimpse into the realities of teen parenthood from a boy's perspective.

Cart, Michael, Ed. *Love & Sex: Ten Stories of Truth.* **New York: Simon & Schuster Books for Young Readers. 2001.**
Each of the 10 stories in this book has to do with love and sex among teens. Two of the short stories are relevant to the topic of pregnancy. The first story "Extra Virgin" by Joan Bauer is about Beth, an 18-year-old teen committed to abstinence. As long as she dates boys like Leonard Flickers, her decision has been easy. However, when Cal Fedders walks into the ice cream shop and orders two scoops of coconut ice cream from her, her commitment to abstinence becomes much more difficult. The second story, "Fine and Dandy," by Louise Hawes is about Casey and her very loyal and trustworthy beau Pratt Nolan. Like many teens, their first sexual encounter is rooted in curiosity. While watching the video "Madame Bovary," Casey decides that she must break up with Pratt, or she will end up doomed like Madame Bovary in a loveless marriage. Within a few weeks, Beth's suspicion that she might be pregnant is confirmed by a pregnancy test kit purchased at the drug store. Casey briefly considers marrying Pratt and having the child, even though she wants to go to college. In this short story, it is Pratt who would have welcomed the child whereas Beth knows she is not ready. "Fine and Dandy" will spark interesting discussions about the rights of fathers.

Dessen, Sarah. *Someone Like You.* **New York: Viking Childrens Books. 1998.**
Michael Alex Sherwood died on August 13 at 8:55 p.m. after a businessman driving a BMW knocks him off the motorcycle he has only owned since June. Michael died not knowing that his girlfriend, Scarlett Thomas, was pregnant. This love story between Scarlett and Michael deals with her decision to raise the baby on her own. Scarlett's mother is pressuring her to have an abortion because she knows firsthand how difficult it is to be a teenage mother. Even though Scarlett's life has been very unconventional and difficult, and oftentimes she has had to be the adult in the family, she realizes that she is alive because her mother made the decision not to abort her.

Fienberg, Anna. *Borrowed Light.* **New York: Dell Laurel-Leaf. 1999.**
Sixteen-year-old Callisto May has had to be the adult in her dysfunctional family. Her mother is emotionally absent and her father is a workaholic. When Callisto becomes pregnant, she knows that she is on her own with no one to rely on. Even when Callisto goes to the family planning clinic for an abortion, she has to take Jeremy, her younger brother, with her because her mother is busy attending her weekly New Age therapy group. The abortion precipitates a family emergency when Jeremy turns up missing. A family secret is finally revealed, and Callisto is able to talk to her parents about her needs.

Hrdlitschka, Shelley. *Dancing Naked.* **Custer, WA: Orca Book Publishers. 2001.**
Sixteen-year-old Kia does not know how to tell her parents she is pregnant. Although Kia suspects her boyfriend would be unsupportive, she never imagines

he would become so hateful toward her. When Kia declines to abort the baby, her boyfriend refuses to admit he is the father. Kia is devastated. For support, Kia turns to her church group. The group's leader, Justin, becomes Kia's childbirth coach. During her pregnancy, Kia meets Grace, an elderly woman who is dying of cancer, who helps her believe in herself again. At first, Kia wants to keep the baby; but eventually she realizes she is not ready to assume responsibility for another human being.

Pennebaker, Ruth. *Don't Think Twice.* **New York: Henry Holt and Company. 1996.**
Back in the 1950s when girls like Anne Harper became pregnant, they were mysteriously shipped off only to reappear nine months later. Anne is the kind of daughter that parents do not worry about. She rarely dated and she seemed too smart for something like this to happen. Parts of *Don't Think Twice* are laugh-out-loud humorous as Anne recounts the antics of the girls who are locked up in this Texas home for pregnant teens. Other parts of the book are tragic as Anne writes about the girls' dysfunctional families, the pain that is felt because their boyfriends refuse to take responsibility, and the mourning that occurs when the babies are taken away right after birth.

Plummer, Louise. *A Dance for Three.* **New York: Dell Laurel-Leaf. 2000.**
When Milo finds out his 15-year-old girlfriend, Hannah Ziebarth, is pregnant with his baby, he vehemently denies paternity, beats her up, and spreads vicious rumors that she is a whore. Hannah is desperate because her own home life is crumbling. She had hoped that Milo and his family would take her in and make her part of their family. Because of her mother's depression, Hannah has had to assume all responsibilities for the home and the welfare of her mother. Although the pregnancy leads to Hannah's breakdown and subsequent placement in a mental institution, it is the catalyst that gets help for her mother. By the time the baby is born and adopted out, Hannah and her mother are on their way to being healed.

Porter, Connie. *Imani All Mine.* **New York: Houghton Mifflin Company. 1999.**
Tasha is the 14-year-old mother of a baby girl named Imani. She is overwhelmed by the monotonous routine of preparing bottles and changing diapers. Her school experience in a special class for teen mothers is described in detail. Tasha is struggling to be a mother even though she lives in a ghetto where there are few resources. Poverty, racism, and danger confront her daily. After Imani's birth, Tasha begins a sexual relationship with Peanut and becomes pregnant again. There is a good role model in the African-American woman doctor who speaks harshly to Tasha about the frequency of teen pregnancy and how children like her should not be having children. This book contains some graphic language.

Williams-Garcia, Rita. *Like Sisters on the Homefront.* **New York: Lodestar Books. 1995.**
Fourteen-year-old Gayle is every parent's worst nightmare. Gayle already has one child by a married man, and she is pregnant with another. She has few academic skills and has no interest in education. She is surrounded by drugs, sexual

opportunities, and school failure. Gayle's mother fears that if her daughter continues in this environment, she will never be able to turn her life around and have a future. When Gayle becomes pregnant again, her mother forces her to have an abortion and immediately afterward puts her on the plane to live with her stern uncle, a minister, and his college professor wife hoping that they can straighten her out. As Gayle learns about her family's history she begins to have hope for her future.

Wolff, Virginia Euwer. *Make Lemonade*. **New York: Henry Holt and Company. 1993.** This first book in the *Make Lemonade* trilogy is delightful and uplifting. Set in an impoverished inner city neighborhood, LaVaughn's mother is her daughter's greatest cheerleader. She makes many sacrifices so that LaVaughn can go to college and escape the poverty in which she has grown up. But LaVaughn needs a job and the one she finally accepts is to take care of the two children of a 17-year-old teen mother named Jolly who is a magnet for bad luck. LaVaughn eventually talks Jolly into enrolling in a high school program for teen mothers. Told in narrative poetry, this book takes the reader into the life of poverty of a teenage mother who is locked into minimum wage jobs. Jolly is able to turn her life around and LaVaughn stays true to her goal of going to college. In the second book of the trilogy, *True Believer*, LaVaughn's mother continues to encourage her daughter to attend college even though LaVaughn becomes temporarily sidetracked by a romantic love interest and considers having her first sexual relationship.

Chapter Eleven

Relationship Violence

Nearly one-third of all teens in America say that either they or a friend have experienced dating violence. To bring attention to this significant problem, the clothing manufacturer Liz Claiborne has developed a Web site to warn teens about patterns of relationship abuse and violence through the story of Angela and Joe, a fictional teen couple (*What You Need to Know about Dating Violence* 4–22). In this relationship, Joe has become controlling of Angela's time and attention. He demands to know where she is, what she is doing, and who she is with. Although Angela is concerned about the speed at which the relationship is developing and its exclusivity, she does not know what to do.

> "When he hit me, I didn't see it coming. It was just a quick blur, a flash out of the corner of my eye, and then the side of my face just exploded, burning, as his hand slammed against me."—*Dreamland* by Sarah Dessen

Through Angela and Joe's story, teens learn that dating violence may take the form of jealousy, damaging possessions, saying things to hurt feelings, making insults in front of others, trying to control, threatening, scratching, slapping, kicking, biting, choking, pushing, and grabbing. Sexual coercion is one form of relationship violence (Advocates for Youth, par. 1). Studies show that the incidence of unwanted sex is high for both males and females (Zimmerman et al. 385). In another study, Cascardi, Avery-Leaf, and O'Leary found that 32% of males and 52% of females had used aggression against a dating partner (James et al. 567).

Signs of potential violence in a perpetrator are:

- Being abused as a child;
- Frequent loss of temper;
- A violent attitude;
- Drunkenness or drug abuse;

- Possessiveness; and
- Strict traditional ideas about the roles of men and women (James et al. 567).

Parents and educators should be concerned about teen girls if they notice any of the following:

- The teen girl is overly worried about upsetting her boyfriend or making him angry;
- She foregoes activities that were once important to her and is becoming more and more isolated;
- Her weight, appearance, or grades have changed dramatically — these changes may be signs of depression, which could indicate abuse; and
- She has injuries she cannot explain (*What You Need to Know About Dating Violence* 9).

One of the most violent forms of relationship violence is rape. This is defined as a sexual assault in which a person uses his penis or other object to commit vaginal, oral, or anal penetration of a victim by force or threat of force. Rape is committed against the victim's will, or when the victim is physically or mentally unable to give consent. Most often the perpetrators are male; the victims are female. Date rape is rape that happens between two partners who are dating. Acquaintance rape is rape that happens when the victim and the perpetrator are acquainted. (Lindquist 3).

Research conducted by Mary P. Koss and published in *Ms. Magazine* in 1985 brought national attention to the issue of acquaintance rape. Funded by the National Institute of Mental Health, her research debunked the myth that sexual advances and intercourse were not rape if perpetrator and victim know each other (Curtis 9). Koss surveyed over 6,000 college-age men and women about sexual aggressiveness they had experienced. Of the 3,187 women surveyed, one in four reported that she had been the recipient of some form of sexual aggressiveness. Fifteen percent reported that they had been raped. Of this number, 84% had known their victim. Even though 96% of the victims told a friend about the rape, only 2% of the female rape victims reported the crime to the police (Warshaw ix).

Similar research conducted by Suzanne S. Ageton of the Behavioral Research Institute found that nearly all teenage rape victims knew their attackers. She found that while 71% of the victims confided in their teen friends, 78% did not tell their parents about the rape and only 6% reported the rape to the police (Warshaw 119). The reasons for not telling parents or authorities after acquaintance rape are:

- Fear of not being believed because the perpetrator may be well known and popular;
- The disbelief that the perpetrator must rape in order to have intercourse;
- Victims may not recognize that the sexual aggression is rape — they blame themselves because they feel "betrayed by their own judgment because men that they know, men whom they have often been attracted to, men they have sometimes chosen have turned on them in such a terrible way" (Warshaw 56); and
- The victim may be hesitant to tell authorities because the incident might

have involved illegal drinking and drug use, going to a place that was forbidden, or previous sexual activity (125).

The effects of acquaintance rape may actually be more severe than rape committed by a stranger. The consequences of acquaintance and date rape are more emotional because the victim may not be believed. The victim may be shunned, scared, or harassed by the perpetrator. Other emotional consequences may be depression, anxiety, and complications in subsequent relationships. Some teens may become shy and withdrawn while others may act out sexually and become promiscuous. Survivors of acquaintance and date rape must acknowledge the aggression, discuss it with parents, friends, and the authorities, find help, and educate themselves about prevention strategies (Curtis, pars. 19–22).

Many date and acquaintance rapes are often planned. First, the perpetrator gets to know the victim long enough for her to let down her guard. Second, the perpetrator devises a plan to be with the victim in an isolated place where escape is difficult (Gedatus 10). Third, alcohol and drugs are often involved. It is estimated that 75% of males and over half the females were drunk at the time of the rape (Lindquist 39). Being drunk or high may cause the perpetrator to become more aggressive and the victim to have diminished responsiveness and judgment (Warshaw 121). Because alcohol and drugs break down inhibitions and the inner code of behavior, teens might do things while they are drunk or high that they would not do otherwise. Alcohol mixed with drugs might cause the victim to pass out and become vulnerable to aggression. In addition, a girl who gets drunk may falsely depend on her friends to keep her safe (Lindquist 40). Teens are especially vulnerable to rape because so much of the high school social scene and culture is centered around drugs and alcohol (Warshaw 121).

Some drugs are being used to facilitate rape. One such drug, Rohypnol, most commonly called "Roofies," or the date rape drug, is a powerful sedative which is commonly prescribed as a sleeping pill in Europe and Latin America. Rohypnol tablets are round, white, and slightly smaller than an aspirin; they often come packaged in a bubble wrap container that gives them the appearance of legitimate medicine. Rohypnol causes drowsiness, loss of inhibition and judgment, dizziness, confusion, and amnesia. The tablets dissolve easily in beverages, such as soft drinks, beer, and liquor. They leave no taste, color, or odor and take effect within minutes of being ingested. "Roofies" are often combined with alcohol, marijuana, or cocaine to produce a rapid and very dramatic "high." Even when used by themselves, "Roofies" can cause users to exhibit the symptoms of intoxication such as slurred speech, loss of coordination, swaying, and blood-shot eyes (Lindquist 48).

A second drug, GHB or Gamma Hydoxybutrate, was developed in the 1980s as a surgical anaesthetic. GHB is a liquid that comes packaged in small bottles. When combined with alcohol, GHB acts as a sedative that causes memory loss, loss of consciousness, tiredness, vertigo, reduced heart rate, seizures, respiratory failure, and even coma. GHB is particularly dangerous when combined with alcohol. A third drug, Ketamine, sometimes called "Special K," causes feelings of detachment, confusion, and lack of coordination. Mixing this drug with alcohol is very dangerous (Lindquist 50).

Another cause of rape is poor communication and incorrect perceptions. Some perpetrators may perceive certain clothing as being an invitation to rape. Sometimes perpetrators may believe that if they spend money on their dates, they are entitled to sex. While rape is never justified, experts say that teens need to clearly communicate to their dating partners what they expect from the date.

Men who commit rape often do so in order to establish power over a woman through sexually aggressive behavior. They know that they can get away with the aggression because either the victim will not report the crime, proof will come down to "he said she said," or they do not understand that "No" means no. A well-known lecturer on rape, Scott Lindquist, states, "In a recent seminar at a prominent university fraternity in Georgia, I was amazed at the attitude of the men I was addressing. When asked, "How many 'No's' does it take before you finally stop your sexual pursuit?" the answer was, 'Twenty or thirty' " (Lindquist 5).

The key steps in preventing acquaintance and date rape are to:

- Avoid men who have a reputation for acquaintance rape, berating women, drinking heavily, and acting intimidating;
- Be assertive and act immediately to say "No;"
- Stay sober because alcohol and drugs are a contributing factor to acquaintance and date rape;
- Find out about the person before the date—parental neglect and sexual and physical abuse in childhood are linked to a propensity to rape;
- Remain in control—teens might consider paying their own way (some men think that sex is to be offered in exchange for dinner or a movie) or driving to the date alone so that leaving at any time is an option;
- Stay away from isolated places; and
- Trust the little voice of intuition that says something is not right (Wolfe et al. 286).

Relationship Violence Books for Middle School Readers

Sparks, Beatrice. *It Happened to Nancy.* **New York: Avon Books. 1994.**
This book recounts the date rape of Nancy, a 14-year-old, by a child predator. When an attractive young man at a Garth Brooks concert helps rescue Nancy from a scuffle in which her purse is stolen, she immediately trusts him and lets down her guard. This naïve and inexperienced teen is won over by his flowers and kind words. Eventually, Nancy invites him over to her house for dinner and he rapes her. As a result of the rape, Nancy develops AIDS and dies within months.

Relationship Violence Books for High School Readers

Anderson, Laurie Halse. *Speak.* **New York: Farrar, Straus and Giroux. 1999.**
In eighth grade, Melinda was a happy-go-lucky student who made B's in her classes and had many friends. All that changed the night she attended an end-of-

summer party featuring beer, seniors, and music. Instead of friends and B's, she spends her freshman year in high school shunned by other students. Told in four chapters, each representing one term of her freshman year, readers experience Melinda's pain, her inability to communicate what happened at the party, and what it must feel like to be shunned and harassed. What went wrong at the party was that Melinda was raped by senior Andy Evans, a notoriously fast boy. At the time that she was raped, Melinda, who was not used to alcohol, was drunk. She feels guilty because she was not able to yell, "Stop!" Melinda cannot talk to anybody. What starts to bring her around is the suggestion that Andy had done this kind of thing before. When Melinda writes on the bathroom stall that Andy Evans is dangerous, soon the whole wall is filled with anti-Andy comments. When Andy tries to rape her again, she struggles and is able to yell, "No." The only person in the story who is even remotely sympathetic to her, and guesses that something must have happened, is her art teacher. The power of art helps Melinda express her pain.

Dessen, Sarah. *Dreamland*. New York: Puffin Books. 2000.
This is a beautifully written story about Caitlin O'Korem and her vulnerability following a family crisis which leaves her susceptible to the charms of bad boy Rogerson Briscoe. Caitlin is intrigued with Rogerson's life, although their dates consist mostly of her accompanying him while he's taking care of business—in this case, a lucrative drug trade. The first time she sees Rogerson's father hit him over a small infraction, Caitlin feels so nurturing and needed as she comforts him. However, soon Rogerson is hitting her just like his father hits him. She changes from a happy-go-lucky teen to one who is depressed, anxious, sleeps in class, and is experiencing academic failure. Eventually a neighbor witnesses Rogerson hitting Caitlin and calls the police. Caitlin is hospitalized for treatment—technically for drugs—to learn how to stand up for herself. This book shows how easily a teenage girl can become isolated and fall under the spell of a controlling boyfriend.

Flinn, Alex. *Breathing Underwater*. New York: HarperCollins Publishers. 2001.
This must-buy book is written from the perspective of a teen male who is abusing his sweetheart. After Nick hits Caitlin, she has him arrested. The judge orders him to attend six months of violence and anger management counseling. Because he does not comprehend that he did anything wrong, the judge also requires him to keep a journal about his relationship with Cailtin. Intermingled with his description of counseling and the shunning he receives once his abuse of Caitlin is made known is the story of his own abuse at the hands of his father. This is an intriguing book that teens love.

Miklowitz, Gloria D. *Past Forgiving*. New York: Simon & Schuster Books for Young Readers. 1995.
At 15, Alexandra is thrilled to be dating Cliff, a handsome and athletic senior. Even from the very beginning of their relationship, there are signs that that he is controlling and abusive. Within weeks of beginning to date, Cliff becomes possessive, abusive, and eventually rapes Alexandra when he gets tired of waiting for sex.

Stratton, Allan. *Leslie's Journal.* **Toronto: Firefly Books. 2000.**

Leslie Phillips, a high school junior, has had a difficult time ever since she and her family moved from Seattle and her parents divorced. Except for Katie, she has never found a clique of her own. All this makes her ripe for the attention of the new bad boy at school, a motorcycle driving senior named Jason McCready. On their first date, Leslie gets drunk and is raped. Jason is suave and says just the right things to keep Leslie in this abusive and physical relationship. Eventually Katie notices all the bruises on Leslie and convinces her that she needs to leave this relationship. Getting out is not so easy. Leslie files stalking charges against Jason only to find out that he has done this to other girls as well. As a result, one girl committed suicide. Because Leslie's experiences are recorded in her journal for English class, she is able to prove the abuse and stalking charges.

Chapter Twelve

Driving

After downing a few beers in *Tears of a Tiger* by Sharon Draper, the high school basketball players drove off amid much jocularity to savor Robert's 27 points and the win. Life couldn't get much better for these guys. Within the hour though, Robert would die pinned to his seat as the small red Chevette burst into flames. Maybe Barry Cox in *I Know What You Did Last Summer* by Lois Duncan would have seen the 10-year-old boy on his bicycle if he hadn't been drinking and smoking weed that evening. Even though Robert and Barry are fictional characters, real-life versions of their stories take place every day in this country. In fact, a 16-year-old is more than 20 times more likely to have a crash than any other licensed driver. Automobile crashes are the leading cause of death in 15–20 year olds (NHTSA 1).

> "Kids," said the cop, shrugging. He had seen it before, he would see it again. "They don't think. They like the shape of stop signs, you know. We hafta replace 'em all the time. Kids probably figure whoever's driving here will figure it out. You know, stop whether the sign's there or not. Kids don't stop to think. They forget that eventually it's the middle of the night. No traffic. No clues. This Denise Thompson, she's a stranger to the road, she needs the stop sign." — *Driver's Ed* by Caroline B. Cooney

Teens in America eagerly await the day they will pass their driver's test, pose for the camera, and receive the laminated card that represents to them freedom and independence. Within the year though, one in three of these teens will have a crash resulting from his or her lack of driving experience and skill (AmISafe? par. 3). When teens crash, their injuries tend to be more severe because they are less likely to use seat belts, they are more likely to speed and drive drunk, and they often drive small cars that are less safe in a crash (Ponton 207). The National Highway Traffic Safety Administration (NHTSA) estimates that in 2000, 69% of teens involved in fatal crashes had been drinking and were not wearing seatbelts (NHTSA 5).

When teens drink and drive, they are more likely than adults to crash—even when drinking less alcohol. Nearly one-third of teen driving fatalities involve alcohol use. All states and the District of Columbia now have 21-year-old minimum drinking age laws in place. According to estimates by the NHTSA, these laws have made a difference. Since 1975, the NHTSA estimates that minimum drinking age laws have saved 20,043 teen lives (5).

A second contributing factor to teen driving fatalities and injuries is nighttime driving, which is more difficult and challenging for novice drivers. As a group, teenagers drive fewer cumulative hours than adults, but they drive disproportionately more at night and have a much higher nighttime crash fatality rate. A teen is more than four times more likely to be killed while driving at night than during the day (The "Teenage Driver" 987). Weekends are another deadly time for teens. Fifty-five percent of all teen motor vehicle deaths occur on Friday, Saturday, or Sunday. During a typical weekend, an average of one teenager dies each hour in an automobile crash. Thirty-five percent of these deaths occur between the hours of 9 p.m. and 3 a.m. Statistics show that cities that institute night curfews have lowered teen injuries and fatalities by as much as 23% (Runyan and Gerken 2276).

Automobile crashes among teens have become such a problem that many states are considering, or have passed, legislation to strengthen penalties for teenagers caught driving drunk. An example of stiffer legislation is Sean's Law, which is named after a 17-year-old Columbia County, New York, track star who died in a car crash on New Year's Eve 2001. Although the teenager who was driving the car had recently failed a sobriety test, he was allowed to keep his license and continue to drive since he had not yet appeared at his court date. Now, judges in New York are required to immediately suspend the licenses of teens caught driving drunk (Dewan B5).

Another way that states are fighting back is by passing the three tiered "graduated license" laws. These laws require novice teen drivers to obtain a learner's permit and then an intermediate or provisional license before earning their regular driver's license. Teens with learner's permits and provisional licenses may have their nighttime driving curtailed, may not be able to chauffeur other teens, and may be required to undergo more supervised training ("The Teenage Driver" 990).

The American Academy of Pediatrics believes the prevention of automobile crashes requires multiple strategies such as requiring teens to use seat belts, instituting nighttime driving curfews, passing legislation to increase the legal drinking age, stiffening the penalties for teens who drive, drink, and use drugs, and upping the age requirement for obtaining an unrestricted driver's license ("The Teenage Driver" 989). In addition, adults and parents can help by becoming aware of their states' teen driving laws. The NHTSA estimates that 41% of the driving public is not knowledgeable about teen driving laws (MADD, par. 22). Information about state driving laws is available on the Internet at the DriveHomeSafe.com Web site at <http://www.drivehomesafe.com/just_4_u_teens.htm>.

Neuroscientists say that because the skills associated with maturity are not fully developed in the prefrontal cortex part of the teen's brain until about 20 years of age, "many of the reasonings of the adult might not make sense to a teen because they haven't developed complex abstract thinking" says Dr. David Kristl, a South Bend, Indiana, neurologist (Rumbach, par. 25). The "Don't Drink and Drive" messages may be ineffective unless delivered in a format that is meaningful to teens. He suggests that driving messages be repeated often, be real, and "cut straight to the bottom line" such as a smashed-up car placed on the lawn of the high school before prom (par. 27).

Driving Books for Middle School Readers

Cooney, Caroline. *Driver's Ed.* **New York: Bantam Doubleday Books for Young Readers. 1994.**

Street signs are stolen all the time; however, in this book, teens come face-to-face with the consequences of an evening of sign stealing. A suggestion is made during driver education class that they take street signs. The intent was to just take street signs that they could hang in their bedrooms, but somehow the stop sign at the intersection of Warren and Cherry was also stolen. As a result, the inevitable happened. "Last night a fatal car accident occured... A car driven by 26-year-old Denise Thompson was hit broadside by a truck. Denise Thompson was killed instantly" (68). *Driver's Ed* is a realistic and readable book that draws readers into the emotions felt by the sign stealers. This book has many teachable passages that can be used to promote critical thinking and decision making. An absolute must read for driver education students and all teens who drive.

Tomey, Ingrid. *Nobody Else Has to Know.* **New York: Dell Laurel-Leaf. 1999.**

In this book, 15-year-old Webber's grandfather thinks that it is all right to let his grandson drive even though he has not taken the required driver's education course and does not have a learner's permit. Webber has driven many times accompanied by his grandfather in the passenger's seat. On this day, though, Webber is fiddling with the radio when he loses control of the car he is driving and hits a young girl. She is in a coma and will never walk again. When Webber wakes up in the hospital with a broken leg and a concussion, he does not remember the accident. His grandfather takes the blame. Slowly, Webber begins to remember. Now he has to decide whether to tell the truth or not.

Driving Books for High School Readers

Draper, Sharon M. *Tears of a Tiger.* **New York: Atheneum. 1994.**

The obituary reads: "Teen Basketball Star Killed in Fiery Crash. Nov. 8—Robert Washington, age 17, captain of the Hazelwood High School basketball team, was killed last night in a fiery automobile accident on I-75. Witnesses say the car, driven by Andrew Jackson, 17, also of the Hazelwood team, had been noticeably weaving across the lanes of the expressway just before it hit a retaining wall and burst into flames" (1). The first 18 pages describe the accident, how it happened, and its effect on Robert's friends. This is a very readable book that touches on other issues such as race and suicide. *Tears of a Tiger* traces Andy's reaction to the crash through police interviews, letters by his classmates, articles, homework assignments, and conversations.

Duncan, Lois. *I Know What You Did Last Summer.* **New York: Pocket Books. 1973.**

Barry, Helen, Ray, and Julie had been out partying that summer evening. They had been drinking beer and smoking marijuana. As usual, Barry was driving too fast. He was more interested in Helen than the road. After running down a 10-year-old boy on his bicycle, Barry does not want to stop and help the boy because he is 18 years old and could be tried as an adult. A mystery develops as the dead boy's brother methodically tracks down the teens to avenge the death. Many students may be familiar with this book because it was released as a movie in 1997.

Fleischman, Paul. *Whirligig*. New York: Henry Holt and Company, Inc. 1998.
Brent Bishop has spent much of his life moving from city to city and school to school, always trying to be popular with each new group of students. He is invited to a party and starts drinking hoping that this will help him relax and be more social. But instead he becomes obnoxious. On the way home from the party, he intended to end his life, but instead crashed into the car driven by 18-year-old Lea Rosalia Santos Zamora and killed her. As restitution, Lea's mother requests that Brent make four whirligigs, Lea's favorite wooden toy. These whirligigs are to be painted to look like Lea and placed in Washington, California, Florida, and Maine so that "people all over the country receive joy from her even though she's gone" (41). This book recounts Brent's 45 days traveling around the country making the whirligigs and changing lives. Brent learns a universal truth: good deeds survive and change all those they touch.

Keizer, Garret. *God of Beer*. New York: HarperCollins Publishers. 2002.
God of Beer is more fully reviewed in the chapter on Substance Abuse, but this book has an unusual death of a designated driver, Diana LaValley, the 6'4" lead scorer on the basketball team. Diana attends a weekend party, but she is not drinking. However, Condor, Diana's boyfriend, has been drinking heavily. All evening Diana has had to push Condor away because he becomes very amorous and groping after he has been drinking. Eventually she drives Condor home because he is too drunk to drive himself. Nobody really knows what happened, but a witness on the interstate tells the police that he had seen "what looked like a struggle." The message about designated drivers usually revolves around preserving the life of the drinker, but what about the safety of the designated driver? This scene at the beginning of Part 3 can be used to discuss the safety of the designated driver while chauffeuring someone who is drunk or drugged and may be out of control.

Orr, Wendy. *Peeling the Onion*. New York: Bantam Doubleday Dell Books for Young Readers. 1996.
Hayden was simply driving his girlfriend home from a karate tournament when Trevor Jones collides with them. Hayden and Trevor walk away, but Anna will never be the same. This very readable book is about Anna's slow and painful recovery and her realization that she will never again be the athletic, beautiful, and easy-go-lucky teen she once was. Even though Anna's perfect and carefree existence was snuffed out in the crash, her life, which is forever changed, will continue. Passages from this book could be read and discussed with teens to help them understand the importance of driving defensively. This book shows how life can change in an instant just by being in the wrong place.

Voigt, Cynthia. *Izzy Willy-Nilly*. New York: Atheneum. 1986.
Isobel Lingard is an athletic, pretty, and popular high school freshman, who con-

vinces her reluctant parents to let her go to a party with Marco, a senior. At the party, Marco drinks too much but insists on driving Izzy home. On the way, he runs into a tree and passes out. If he had not passed out, Izzy might have received medical attention sooner and not lost her leg. Other students at the party knew how drunk Marco was and feel guilty that they did not stop him from driving Izzy home that night. Besides losing a leg, Izzy, a member of a popular clique, finds out how shallow her friends are as they desert her one by one. Only Rosamunde, a strange and socially inept girl, stands by Izzy. They develop a warm and mature friendship that is not based on appearances and cliques.

Chapter Thirteen

Bullying and Cliques

It used to be that bullying was dismissed as a normal part of childhood, but school shootings at Columbine and elsewhere have focused national attention on the connection between bullying and violence. Bullying, the most prevalent form of violence among teens, is defined as a specific form of aggressive behavior which is intended to harm or disturb and occurs repeatedly over time; usually there is an imbalance of power between the bully and the victim (Nansel et al. 2094; Olson 93). Bullying is all about power. Bullies use physical, verbal, and emotional or psychological methods to humiliate, embarrass, or overpower someone who is more vulnerable. Bullying occurs at all ages, in all social groups, and knows no financial, cultural, or social bounds. What differentiates bullying from playing around is the intent of the interaction and the relationship between the bully and the victim. Bulling behavior typically includes:

- Kicking, hitting, pushing, spitting, or other forms of physical abuse;
- Taunting, teasing, name-calling, making malicious comments, or deliberately isolating someone;
- Spreading rumors, telling lies, or deliberately setting someone up to get into trouble;
- Taking or stealing things from someone;
- Forcing or pressuring someone to do something he or she does not want to do; or
- Sexually harassing someone in any way (Huebner and Morgan, par. 3).

> "Because they're scared of him," Roy said. Which was also why none of the other kids had backed up his story. Nobody wanted to nark on Dana and have to face him the next day on the bus.
> —*Hoot* by Carl Hiaasen

During the spring of 1998, the National Institute of Child Health and Human Development (NICHHD) surveyed 15,686 students in grades six through 10 in public and private schools throughout the United States to measure the prevalence of bullying and its association with problem behavior (Nansel et al. 2094). The study revealed that nearly one in three students participates in bullying either as a bully, victim, or both. In addition, bullying occurs more frequently among sixth to eighth grade students than ninth and tenth graders, and students involved in bullying have more behavioral and adjustment problems than other teens. In a study conducted by the U.S. Department of Education, it was reported that 77% of middle and high school students in a small Midwestern town had been bullied (Garbarino and deLara 1).

The National Education Association estimates that 160,000 students miss school every day due to fear of attack or intimidation by a bully. Other research shows that 10% of teens who drop out do so because of repeated bullying and that 90% of all students believe that bullying causes social, emotional, or academic problems for students who are bullied (Weinhold, par. 22). Although many students can withstand being bullied, students who are not as resilient may experience shame, lessened self-esteem, impaired self-image (Garbarino and deLara 25), depression, and suicide (82). In addition, in a study conducted by the American Association of Suicidology, 20% of high school students said that they had seriously considered attempting suicide in the preceding 12 months. The main triggers for committing suicide are teasing, bullying, and social rejection (Middleton-Moz and Zawadski 5).

Students who do not feel safe at school because they are afraid of being bullied and harassed may attempt to "solve" their problem in ways that actually limit their academic and personal development. For instance, students may not contribute to class discussions or try to get good grades because they fear they will be bullied for being intelligent. They may not participate in clubs and sports because of hazing. They may feel "sick" at recess or gym class to avoid being bullied by the more athletic students. They may be afraid to eat in the cafeteria or use the restroom because these are places that are often unsupervised and notorious for bullying. They may become involved in a premature relationship as protection against sexual harassment. They may join a group or gang for protection. Finally, teens may use drugs to dull the hurt and shame of being bullied (Garbarino and deLara 17).

Research on European and Australian teens, along with the NICHHD study, indicates that even though the amount of bullying varies among countries, the type of bullying is very constant. Direct physical aggression is more common among boys, while indirect forms of bullying are more common among girls (Nansel et al. 2094). The type of bullying commonly employed by girls, called "relational aggression," includes spreading rumors, telling lies, manipulating by threatening not to maintain the friendship, and using their popularity to cause a girl to be shunned. Girls' bullying may go unnoticed and unstopped because it seems so civil compared to the more physical and boisterous forms of bullying in which boys engage. Because relational aggression may be accomplished quietly through whispered threats and shunning, teachers and other adults may not even recognize it is occurring (Simmons 21).

In a longitudinal study spanning 35 years, a University of Michigan psychologist found that children who were labeled bullies by other students at age eight often continued with this behavior throughout their lives (*More Information on Bullying*, par. 21). Children do not simply outgrow bullying behavior but instead become better over time at what they do. To end the behavior, bullies must receive "consistent intervention, compassionate confrontation and consequences" and become accountable for their actions (Middleton-Moz and Zawadski 9).

Some children become bullies as a reaction to the violence they experience at home. When they get hurt at home, they come to school and look for someone on which to pass this hurt. Other children view bullying as "payback" time for the bullying they have experienced. Bullying may be cultural in nature. Cultural bullying may involve hazing and harassment by dominant social groups—like athletes. Bullying that is a part of the culture of the school is often tolerated by adults (Garbarino and deLara 72). In order to stop bullying, schools must change their cultures and present a clear message that violence will not be accepted. Schools can do this by supporting character education, teaching students to accept and appreciate diversity, and encouraging students to get to know each other, thereby minimizing the fearfulness of difference (65).

Many different types of teens are targets of bullies. Tom Brown, filmmaker and founder of the "Broken Toy Project," an effort to raise awareness about the issues of bullying and teasing, asked teens to tell him who gets bullied. They replied fat kids, skinny kids, boys who "suck" in sports, boys who act like "fags," lesbians, kids who are smart, kids who are dumb, geeks, computer-freaks, kids who wear geeky out-of-style clothes, kids who stink or smell, kids with unkempt hair, teacher's pets, retarded kids, kids who talk funny, minority kids, kids who get poor grades, kids in wheel chairs, kids who get good grades, girls with blonde hair, kids with curly hair, kids with freckles, kids with funny looking ears or noses, and kids with diseases. Children who are perceived as different and lack social skills are more likely to be targets of bullying (Weinhold, pars. 17–19). The kids who were interviewed said that when someone is being bullied, they "run over and watch," but they don't dare intervene lest the attention be turned on them.

Teens who have been bullied may retaliate in anger by wanting to control and hurt others. When William Pollock, author of *Real Boys' Voices*, interviewed Columbine students, they "cast a critical eye on a peer culture that never welcomed Eric or Dylan, a culture of teasing, bullying, and hazing, a culture (similar to cultures elsewhere for boys) that increases emotional disconnection" that had become too much "for two boys who simply never found a place among their peers" (Pollock 175). A study conducted by the National Threat Assessment Center of the U.S. Secret Service concluded that two-thirds of the attackers in 37 school shootings felt that they had been the victims of bullying, threatening, and persecution at the hands of their classmates (Middleton-Moz and Zawadski 7).

According to ABC News, "A major cause of stress at school for children is the fear of being taunted or bullied" (*More Information on Bullying*). Bullying is difficult for schools to combat because teachers and administrators rarely directly witness the bullying behaviors and incidents. Bullying is most likely to occur where adult involvement and supervision is lacking (Olson 94). There are several ways that teachers and administrators can help to curtail bullying:

- Adults who are responsible for establishing a safe school environment must ensure that students are not bullied and harassed. "Telling kids to handle bullying on their own is a dangerous, unfair, and emotionally negligent strategy" (Garbarino and deLara 86);
- All schools are subject to the Safe and Drug Free Schools initiative established by President Clinton. This initiative mandates that American schools do every-

thing in their power to provide a safe environment for all students. More information is available at: <http://www.ed.gov/offices/OESE/SDFS/news.html> or <http://www.schoolsecurity.org>;

- In addition, Title IX of the Education Amendments strives to protect all students from being excluded, denied the benefits of, or subjected to discrimination under any educational program or activity receiving federal financial assistance. One aspect of Title IX is the elimination of sexual harassment in schools. More information is available at: <http://www.ed.gov/offices/OCR/shguide>;
- Adults must stop denying that bullying is happening and receive in-service training on the consequences of bullying, verbal abuse, harassment, and emotional violence (Garbarino and deLara 50);
- Teens need to be taught conflict-resolution skills because violence is never an acceptable way to solve problems (Garbarino and deLara 49);
- There are no bullies without victims. Teens who are bullied should be taught how to stand-up for themselves by developing more pro-social skills (*More Information on Bullying*, par. 32);
- Research shows that a one-on-one connection with an adult, a parent, a teacher, or a coach helps build resiliency in teens (Krovetz 9). Teens who are more resilient are less likely to be involved in bullying;
- The school community must create school and social environments that promote healthy peer interactions and intolerances of bullying (Nansel et al. 2100); and
- Schools might consider uniforms because they will take away "the element of competition among economic classes that kids use to taunt one another" (Garbarino and deLara 65).

Bullying and Clique Books for Middle School Readers

Bloor, Edward. *Tangerine.* **New York: Harcourt Brace & Company. 1997.**
Paul Fisher has never felt safe. He cannot remember a time when he wasn't bullied and harassed by his older brother, Erik, who is destined for football greatness. As long as Erik keeps winning football games by kicking field goals, Paul's parents look the other way, even though it is obvious that Erik is a bully. *Tangerine* is Paul's journal from August 18 through December 6 — a time of great change as he moves with his family from Houston to Tangerine County, Florida. After his school disappears into a sink hole, Paul transfers from upscale Lake Windsor Middle to the older, more racially diverse, and less affluent Tangerine Middle School where he finally learns to fit in. Eventually he remembers what caused his blindness and he accuses his parents of not protecting him.

Deans, Sis. *Racing the Past.* **New York: Henry Holt and Company. 2001.**
Jeffrey Lionel Magee, the legendary character in Jerry Spinelli's *Maniac Magee*, and Ricky Gordon have much in common. Through running they both develop

the self-esteem to cope with their difficult home situations. After Ricky's physically and emotionally abusive father dies in a car accident, he is taunted and teased by Bugsie McCarthy, a sixth grader who threatens to beat him up on the school bus. Because Ricky knows that adults cannot do anything to protect him, he decides that the best thing to is to keep out of Bugsie's way by not riding the school bus. Instead, he runs to and from school. At first it is torture, but soon Rickie falls in love with running. Good things happen to Ricky through running and he is scouted by the high school track coach. *Racing the Past* provides good examples of resiliency as Ricky channels his energy into worthwhile endeavors and finds adults to nurture him.

Hahn, Mary Downing. *Following My Own Footsteps.* **New York: Clarion Books. 1996.**
Following My Own Footsteps is a historical novel set in North Carolina at the end of World War II. After his father is put in jail, Gordy's mother takes the children to stay with their grandmother. Gordy is having a difficult time adjusting to the upscale and civilized surroundings since all he has ever known is abuse, neglect, poverty, and filth. Grandmother is appalled by Gordy's lack of manners, rudeness, and mean spirit. After Gordy almost kills a defenseless boy afflicted with polio, he comes face-to-face with his anger and the reason why he lashes out. With the love and support of his grandmother, Gordy begins to recognize his violent past and make changes. But Gordy's life takes a turn for the worse when his father returns from jail with promises that he has changed.

Hiaasen, Carl. *Hoot.* **New York: Alfred A. Knopf. 2002.**
Hiaasen is known for writing ecological mysteries set in Florida that are chock-full of laugh-out-loud humor and quirky characters. *Hoot* is Hiaasen's first young adult novel. In this story, a developer is ready to bulldoze a vacant lot so that a pancake house can be built. Even though the developer has not had an environmental impact statement prepared, he knows that the lot is the home of a family of hoot owls, a protected species. Intermixed in this environmental story is the bullying that befalls Roy, the new boy in school, at the hands of Dana Matherson, the local bully. Roy is able to use his wits to protect himself from Dana and the hoot owl family from the bulldozer.

Koss, Amy Goldman. *The Girls.* **New York: Dial Books for Young Readers. 2000.**
A definite must buy, Koss takes us into the heart of cliquedom to witness relational aggression at its worst and the cruelty that middle school girls can bestow on each other. Candace, the leader of the clique, has the power to decide who is "in" and who is "out;" what's "hot" and what is "not." Without any provocation, she decides that Maya is definitely out. As if they have no minds of their own, the other girls in the clique, Renée, Darcy, and Brianna, dump Maya, too. Middle school girls will love this book. *The Girls* brings attention to the cruelty of the clique; how shunning, lies, and rumors are forms of bullying; and how girls need to learn to stand up and speak out in their relationships with other girls. At the end of the book, Renée and Darcy apologize to Maya, but Brianna is in the process of being replaced by Nicole.

Singer, Nicky. *Feather Boy.* **New York: Delacorte Press. 2001.**
    If 12-year-old Robert Nobel had been blessed at birth with a body as athletic and fluid as Jonathan Niker's, then maybe his life at school would not be so miserable. Instead, Robert wears glasses that look like the bottoms of two coke bottles and has hair the color and texture of fluffy duck down; his body is thin and gangly. The price he pays for these physical imperfections is daily taunting and teasing at the hands of Jonathan, the class bully.
    Robert is the first in his class to volunteer for a nursing home assignment, the Elders' Project, in which the students and residents of the Mayfield Rest Home share experiences about their childhoods. Through this project, Robert realizes that he is not a scaredy-cat and that Jonathan no longer has power to taunt, tease, and make his life miserable. Chapter 14 is a powerful reminder of what can happen when the bullied teen stands up for himself after he has been pushed once too often.

Bullying and Clique Books for High School Readers

Crutcher, Chris. *Whale Talk.* **New York: Greenwillow Books. 2001.**
    When school administrators and teachers refuse to intervene to stop bullying behavior, then students may take it on themselves to stop the harassment. The result may be Columbine-like school shootings or stories such as *Whale Talk*. In an early scene, Mike Barbour, Cutter High's most talented linebacker, is pushing and intimidating a special education student, Mike Coughlin, because he is wearing a letter jacket that he did not earn, but rather it belonged to his dead brother who was a football legend at the high school. Bullying by Mike and another mean-spirited athlete, Rick Marshall, causes T.J. Jones to put together a swim team of teens who do not fit in for the purpose of earning Cutter High's most highly cultivated prize—the blue and gold letter jacket. The athletic community does everything in its power to ensure that the swim team does not succeed. Because T.J. innately realizes that there are no bullies without victims, he helps each member of the swim team develop his self-esteem and power to rise above the victim persona. This entertaining book should be required reading for anyone who wants to understand the dynamics of an American high school run amuck by a popular and powerful clique.

Flinn, Alex. *Breaking Point.* **New York: HarperTempest. 2002.**
    After his parents divorce, 15-year-old Paul Richmond moves to Miami with his mother, who gets an administrative job at the very exclusive Gate-Brikell Christian School. Paul attends the school on scholarship but soon learns that he is way out of his league in this dangerous place where money rules. Paul who has spent much of his life moving from place to place, and being home schooled, does not possess the social skills to even begin to know how to fit in. This is an amazing story about bullying, harassment, and cruelty. In Paul's case, he is harassed and laughed at, his locker gets trashed and his books ruined, he is tripped, and someone switches the lock on his locker. Although Paul tries to tell his mother and calls his father repeatedly to see if he can go live with him, no

one listens. Life only begins to look up when Charlie Good invites Paul to join his small group of wealthy boys who regularly terrorize neighborhoods, steal, and smash mail boxes. Because of Paul's need for safety, he is powerless to stop himself from being caught up in Charlie's plan to bomb the school.

Gallo, Paul, Ed. *On the Fringe*. New York: Dial Books. 2001.

The dedication of this book sums up its intent: "This book is dedicated to every kid who has ever been called a hurtful name. And to every kid who tried to feel superior by putting down someone else." *On the Fringe* contains 11 short stories written by such popular young adult authors as M.E. Kerr, Jack Gantos, and Chris Crutcher. Between the covers of this book, there are short stories about bullies, the teen victims, and those who retaliate. Two stories bear special notice. In "Geeks Bearing Gifts," by Ron Koertge, Renee, a reporter for the school's newspaper, sets out to interview kids who are different: outcasts, nonconformists, and those that are out of the mainstream. Because Renee has always been a member of the popular clique, interviewing these teens about what they endure at the hands of the "haves" is eye-opening for her. After spending time with these teens, Renee finds that she likes them and chooses to leave her main clique. In another story, "Guns for Geeks" by Chris Crutcher, Gene Taylor has endured a school career of bullying by students and teachers alike. One day he has had enough and methodically strikes back at the teens who have bullied him and a teacher who permitted it.

Koja, Kathe. *Straydog*. New York: Farrar, Straus and Giroux. 2002.

Griffin is not really a chicken, and Rachel is not a dog, but that doesn't stop Jon from making this statement during English class. " 'He's a chicken all right. You should see him in gym'. Jon laughs, Chelsea laughs, Courtney laughs, but Griffin just closes down" (61). Harsh words ensue and a fight develops between the two cliques: the dominator clique comprised of students who think they are so much better than everyone else, and the geek clique with kids like Rachel and Griffin who are angry because they are reminded every day, in one way or another, that they do not belong.

The only place where Rachel fits in is at the animal shelter where she feeds, exercises, and cleans the cages of the cats and dogs that are dropped off or abandoned because they no longer fit into their owners' lifestyles. Rachel becomes especially connected to Grl, an undersocialized and feral collie, and is working on adopting this dog when Grl is euthanized. Interwoven throughout *Straydog* is Rachel's powerful short story about Grl, who like Rachel, has been taunted, teased, and abused by humans.

Plum-Ucci, Carol. *The Body of Christopher Creed*. San Diego: Harcourt Inc. 2000.

This is a fascinating book about Christopher Creed, a high school student who has been bullied and picked on by his classmates because of his annoying ways. His life is even more complicated because Christopher's mother treats him like a drill sergeant, he has no privacy, and he believes that she wants to kill him. Christopher disappears and everyone believes that he committed suicide even though there is nobody to confirm this. The narrator of the book, 16-year-old

Torey Adams, feels guilty because he was one of the teens who tormented Christopher. The power of this book is that it provides the reader a glimpse into the life of a teen who is different. Oftentimes, as in Christopher's case, the lack of social skills is what makes him vulnerable to bullying. However, it is Christopher's intelligence that helps him become a survivor. Readers will have to decide for themselves if Christopher committed suicide or ran away from a dangerous situation.

Strasser, Todd. *Give a Boy a Gun.* **New York: Simon and Schuster Books for Young Readers. 2000.**
Years of being bullied and taunted by athletes and the members of the popular crowd cause Gary Searle and Brandon Lawlor to plan revenge during the school dance at Middletown High. Written as if it were nonfiction, this book interweaves the fictionalized comments of students and teachers as they try to recreate the attack with snippets of factual information about assault guns and school violence. This book delivers a strong message about the connection between school shootings and the availability of assault guns.

Von Ziegesar, Cecily. *Gossip Girl.* **Boston: Little, Brown and Company. 2002.**
If the cable television show "Sex and the City" were rewritten with a relational violence theme and published, the finished product might be this book. Set in a very wealthy and exclusive part of New York City, *Gossip Girl* revolves around the lives of privileged high school girls at the Constance Billard School. Blaire Waldorf has become very used to being the coolest of the cool ever since her best friend, the ultra-gorgeous Serena van der Woodsen, went away to boarding school. After Serena returns from boarding school under questionable circumstances, Blaire knows her social standing is slipping and will do anything in her power to remain the leader of her clique and protect her relationship with Nate.

Part III: Bringing Attention to the Issues

Chapter Fourteen

Calendar of Events

Awareness events can be used by librarians and media specialists to educate teens and adults about specific issues, challenges, and celebrations that affect youth. Adults may elect to publicize these issues in a variety of ways, such as programs, book and realia displays, bulletin boards, Web pages, and newspaper articles. In addition, librarians and media specialists may collaborate with community organizations and individuals to pool their resources for the purpose of bringing attention to the high-risk behaviors identified in this book and promote resiliency in youth. Community organizations play an important role in nurturing and fostering resiliency in three ways: by developing caring environments, by communicating high expectations while providing purposeful support, and by providing ongoing opportunities for meaningful participation (Krovetz 2). In the case of awareness weeks or awareness days, readers will want to contact the sponsoring organization or search the World Wide Web for specific dates, as these may change slightly from year to year. The calendar of events has been organized by month. Within each month, single-day events are identified first, followed by week-long, and then month-long events.

January

Dr. Martin Luther King, Jr. Commemorative Holiday
<http://db.education-world.com/perl/browse?cat_id=4090>

The third Monday of January each year is a time to remember Dr. Martin Luther King's fight for the freedom, equality, and dignity of all races and peoples. A variety of resources about this commemorative day are available on the World Wide Web.

National Hobby Month
<http://www.smarterkids.com/rescenter/library/articles.asp?article=973>

> Hobbies are an important protective factor in building competency and self-esteem. Hobbies provide teens with outlets for creativity and opportunities to work with adult mentors in building social skills.

National Mentoring Month
<http://www.hsph.harvard.edu/chc/mentoringmonth/>

> The goals of National Mentoring Month are to raise awareness of the importance of mentoring, to recruit individuals to mentor, and to encourage organizations to support mentoring.

February

National Eating Disorders Awareness Week
<http://www.nationaleatingdisorders.org/p.asp?WebPage_ID=521>

> The purpose of National Eating Disorders Awareness Week is to draw public and media attention to the problem of eating disorders and body dissatisfaction. This awareness week is held during the second-half of February and is sponsored by the National Eating Disorders Association.

Random Acts of Kindness Week
<http://www.actsofkindness.org/>

> This awareness week, which coincides with Valentine's Day, brings attention to the emotional harm caused by bullying. The sponsor of this awareness week, the Random Acts of Kindness Foundation, has created lesson plans and identified activities that promote psychologically safe environments and help teens expand their social group.

Black History Month
<http://www.kn.pacbell.com/wired/BHM/AfroAm.html>

> In 1926, African-American scholar Carter Godwin Woodson organized the first Negro History Week to bring attention to black history, culture, and achievements. Woodson chose February because it is the month that Frederick Douglass and Abraham Lincoln were born, and it coincides with the anniversary of the founding of the National Association for the Advancement of Colored People. In 1976, this month long celebration was renamed Black History Month.

March

National Self-Injury Awareness Day
<http://www.palace.net/~llama/psych/nsiad.html>

> This grassroots education event is held in early March to bring awareness to the causes and treatment of self-injury. The sponsor of the awareness day is the American Self-Harm Information Clearinghouse.

National Women's History Month
<http://www.nwhp.org/whm/themes/theme03.html>

>The purpose of this month-long celebration is to educate and inspire men and women, young and old, to appreciate one another, to cooperate with each other, and to achieve together. National Women's History Month has its roots in a week-long celebration that was first established in Sonoma County, California, in 1978. The proclamation establishing this celebration can be found at: <http://www.nwhp.org/whm/themes/pres_proclamation02.html>.

April

Alcohol Awareness Month
<http://www.health.org/seasonal/aprilalcohol>

>The National Council on Alcoholism and Drug Dependence sponsors this awareness month to bring attention to drug and alcohol dependence.

Child Abuse Prevention Month
<http://www.calib.com/nccanch/prevmnth/activities/index.cfm>
<http://www.calib.com/nccanch/prevmnth/scope/ques.cfm (in Spanish)>

>In 2000, there were 12.2 victims of abuse per 1,000 children. The purpose of this awareness month is to bring attention to the physical abuse and neglect of children and teens.

Haitian Heritage Month
<http://www.mdpls.org/news/happenings/b_day_cel.asp>
<http://www.dade.k12.fl.us/district1/boarditems/haitianheritage.htm>

>The purpose of this month-long event is to celebrate the historic, cultural, social and economic contributions of Haitians to the United States and the world. The Web article "Double Minority: The Haitians in America" by Bernette A. Mosley-Dozier at <http://www.yale.edu/ynhti/curriculum/units/1989/1/89.01.08.x.html> provides background information about these newcomers to America.

National Poetry Month
<http://www.poets.org/npm/>

>During this month, librarians and media specialists can encourage teens to read and write poetry as an avenue of self-expression to bring awareness to teen issues and concerns.

May

Juneteenth
<http://www.juneteenth.com/whatisjuneteenth.htm>

>June 19th is the oldest worldwide celebration of the ending of slavery. At the Juneteenth Web site there is historical and cultural information about slavery and this celebration.

National Childhood Depression Day
<http://www.nmha.org/children/green/index.cfm>
> It is estimated that one out of every eight children suffers from chronic depression. This awareness day brings attention to bipolar depression, anxiety, and Attention Deficit/Hyperactivity Disorder.

The National Day to Prevent Teen Pregnancy
<http://www.teenpregnancy.org/national/default.asp>
> The purpose of this awareness day is to bring attention to the high rate of teen pregnancy: four out of 10 young women become pregnant at least once by the age of 20.

Turn Beauty Inside Out Day
<http://womensissues.about.com/library/weekly/aa041202a.htm>
> This unusual awareness day is celebrated in mid-May to promote healthy body image and to expand the definition of what makes people beautiful.

Buckle Up America
<http://www.buckleupamerica.org/>
<http://www.cdc.gov/mmwr/preview/mmwrhtml/mm5119a4.htm>
> Teens have the lowest safety belt use among all age groups. This week-long awareness program is sponsored by The National Highway Traffic Safety Administration to bring attention to seat belt safety and the fact that seat belts save lives.

National Suicide Awareness Week
<http://www.mentalhealth.org/highlights/may2002/suicide/>
> Suicide is the third leading cause of death among teens. The purpose of this awareness week, held in mid-May, is to bring attention to the high rate of suicide.

Mental Health Month
<http://www.nmha.org/may/index.cfm>
> Educating the American public about the importance of mental health and the reality of mental illness is the purpose for this awareness month. Sample activities are available at the Web site.

National Asian Pacific Heritage Month
<http://www.cr.nps.gov/nr/feature/asia/>
<http://www.cr.nps.gov/nr/feature/asia/1999/aspac.htm>
> This Web site, sponsored by The National Register of Historic Places, promotes awareness of and appreciation for the historical contributions of Asian and Pacific peoples in the United States and its associated territories.

National Bike Month
<http://www.cdc.gov/ncipc/bike/month.htm>
> Teens who do not exercise are more likely to develop body image problems leading to risky dieting and eating disorders. Researchers believe that exercise releases serotonin, a chemical that modulates mood, emotion, sleep, and appetite.

June

Gay and Lesbian Month
<http://clinton4.nara.gov/WH/New/html/20000602.html>
<http://www.fedglobe.org/issues/pride/pridedoi2002.htm>
> Established by proclamation on June 2, 2000, this awareness month celebrates gender diversity and recognizes contributions of gay and lesbian Americans.

July

You Drink & Drive. You Lose.
<http://www.nhtsa.dot.gov/people/outreach/safesobr/ydydyl/toc.html>
> The purpose of this awareness week is to bring attention to the consequences of driving drunk.

September

International Literacy Day
<http://www.reading.org/meetings/ild/>
> Celebrated in early September, this awareness day brings attention to literacy efforts worldwide. The Center for the Book in the Library of Congress and the International Reading Association cosponsor this event.

Hispanic Heritage Month
<http://latino.sscnet.ucla.edu/heritage/hhhispan.htm>
<http://ssdoo.gsfc.nasa.gov/education/hispanic.html>
> The achievements and heritage of the Hispanic community are promoted during this awareness month.

National Alcohol and Drug Recovery Month
<http://www.mentalhealth.org/Highlights/September2002/nadarm/default.asp>
> Sponsored by the Center for Substance Abuse and Treatment, this awareness month promotes substance abuse treatment and recovery and brings attention to treatment options.

National Library Card Sign-up Month
<http://www.ala.org/pio/librarycard/2001>
> Sponsored by the American Library Association, this awareness month promotes libraries and encourages people to acquire a library card.

October

Lights on After School
<http://www.teenpregnancy.org/about/announcements/events/lightsonafterschool.asp>
> The purpose of this mid-October awareness day is to bring attention to the importance of resiliency-building after-school programs.

National Depression Screening Day
<http://www.mentalhealthscreening.org/depression.htm>
> At this Web site, it is possible to screen oneself for depression and suicide.

National Peer Helpers Day
<http://www.peerhelping.org/NPHADay/NPHADAY.htm>
> This day equips individuals to help others by promoting standards of excellence in peer programs. Because teens with problems often turn to their friends before asking for adult help, this site can be used to help students become mentors to their friends. National Peer Helpers Day is held during Red Ribbon Week.

National Mental Illness Awareness Week
<http://miaw.nami.org/>
> Sponsored by the National Association of Mental Illness, the purpose of this week is to raise awareness of mental illness by celebrating the advances that have been made during the past decade and highlighting the remaining barriers.

Red Ribbon Week
<http://www.tcada.state.tx.us/redribbon/redribbon.html>
> Held in memory of Enrique Camarena, a 37-year-old undercover Drug Enforcement Administration agent who was tortured to death in Mexico in 1985, the purpose of Red Ribbon Week is to battle substance abuse. To honor his death, family and friends started wearing red satin badges.

Domestic Violence Awareness Month
<http://usinfo.state.gov/usa/womrts/dvmonth.htm>
> The purpose of this awareness month is to bring attention to the problem of domestic abuse and its effect on children.

Month of the Young Adolescent
<http://www.nmsa.org/moya/new2002/overview.html>
> Sponsored by the National Middle School Association, this month focuses on the special needs of adolescents aged 10 to 15.

National Disability Employment Awareness Month
<http://www.aapd-dc.org/docs/mentor.html>
> Designed to bring awareness to the problems that disabled people face in the workplace, a key element of this awareness month is National Disability Mentoring Day which promotes the employment of students and job-seekers with disabilities through job shadowing and personal mentoring.

November

Attention Deficit Disorder Month
<http://www.adhd.com/awareness.htm>
> This month brings awareness to the problems of attention deficit disorder and hyperactivity among children, which can be a major cause of educational failure.

National American Indian Heritage Month
<http://www3.kumc.edu/diversity/ethnic_relig/naihm.html>
> In 1999, President Clinton signed the proclamation making November National American Indian Heritage Month. This awareness month brings recognition to the role of the Native American in the development of this country.

National Native American Awareness Month
<http://www.fortunecity.com/victorian/verona/514/14c.html>
> Bringing attention to the indigenous peoples of the world is the purpose of this awareness month. Information about various tribes can be found on the Web site.

National Runaway Prevention Month
<http://www.nrscrisisline.org>
> This prevention month brings attention to the issue of runaway and "throwaway" teens. Every day 1.3 million runaway and homeless youth live on the streets of America. A National Runaway Prevention Curriculum is available to teachers.

December

World AIDS Day
<http://www.worldaidsday.org>
> World AIDS Day is observed on December 1 for the purpose of bringing attention to this illness that affects 40 million people worldwide.

National Drunk and Drugged Driving Prevention Month
<http://ncadd.com/3dmonth/index.htm>
> This awareness month brings attention to the significant problem of impaired driving. More teens die from auto crashes than any other cause, and many of these crashes are the result of alcohol or drug use.

Chapter Fifteen

Interactive Booktalking

Booktalking is a technique used to encourage recreational reading and foster the development of positive reading attitudes (Reeder 5). It is defined as a "formal or informal presentation about a book or group of books designed to entice the listener into reading them" (Chelton 39). A booktalk is an oral "sales pitch for a book" (Reeder 6) that combines "the art of storytelling and salesmanship to demonstrate the pure enjoyment of recreational reading" (15). The inception of booktalking is unclear, but it probably evolved informally from children's story time in libraries. Its first recorded use was at the New York Public Library system in the early 1930s (Reeder 18).

The most prominent figure in the development of booktalking was Margaret A. Edwards, the director of youth services at Baltimore's Enoch Pratt Free Library. First published in 1969, Edwards' book *The Fair Garden and the Swarm of Beasts: The Library and the Young Adult* describes in detail how to plan and deliver booktalks. Edwards trained librarians at Enoch Pratt in booktalk techniques such as voice modulation, facial and hand gestures, eye contact, posture, shifting of feet and stance, tempo and pacing, and strategies to deliver conversations between characters (157–160). According to Edwards, the five objectives of booktalks are to:

- Sell the idea of reading for pleasure;
- Introduce new ideas and new fields of reading;
- Develop appreciation of style and character portrayal;
- Lift the level of reading by introducing the best books the audience can read with pleasure; and
- Humanize books, the library, and librarians (157).

Over time, the techniques of booktalking have been well-established in "how-to" articles published in the library literature. According to Joni Bodart, who has written many practical articles, a booktalk consists of a brief description of the book, which includes information on characters, plot, and setting. The booktalk is often written by the person who is giving the talk. The booktalk is practiced until it can be presented smoothly but is not memorized. Booktalk presentations are often conducted in a school media center, a classroom, or a public library. Presentations usually consist of eight to 15 titles being booktalked. Each title is booktalked for one to five minutes. The optimum presentation length is one class period, or 35 to 45 minutes. Oftentimes, the booktalking session is followed by library or media center announcements about materials, services, and programs that might be of interest to the participants. The last 10 or 15 minutes of a booktalking presentation may be unstructured time so participants can examine books, browse, and ask questions (3–9).

Even though librarians believe that booktalking is effective in promoting recreational reading, there is little empirical evidence to support this other than short-term increases in circulation statistics. Dissertations by Bodart and Gail M. Reeder examined the effect of booktalking on the behavior of readers. "While booktalking is popular, booktalk experts failed to provide conclusive data to demonstrate a relationship between attitude change and booktalking" (Reeder 82). Despite the lack of empirical evidence regarding its long-term effectiveness, booktalking remains a favorite reading promotion technique, and librarians and school media specialists continue to use it.

Now more than ever, educators recognize the importance of promoting and establishing patterns of lifelong reading. Some reluctant readers "have fairly good reading skills; they simply do not like to read. Others are poor readers partly because they get so little practice" (Nilsen and Donelson 346). Whatever the reason, many students do not read well. In response, many middle and high schools offer courses in remedial reading. Many schools provide opportunities for students to read in class in order "to prevent the drop-off in reading that usually occurs when students begin high school, and their social and work schedules leave little time for reading" (347).

Research conducted by Ivey and Broaddus of more than 1,700 students in two geographical areas of the United States indicated that inconsistencies in promoting reading in secondary schools are a cause for student declines in reading. They found that students want to read but because of a mismatch between curricular goals and content requirements and "limited opportunities to explore their own interests in reading, to read at their own pace, or to make their own decisions about whether or not to read a book" (350) they are not supported in their reading attempts.

When Ivey and Broaddus asked middle school students what motivates them to read, they replied "good books" and "many choices" (361). In addition, students liked having teachers read aloud to them. They saw teacher read alouds as helpful in understanding the text and making it more interesting to them.

Even though it is commonly thought that many teens do not value reading, researchers have found that students will read outside of school when it is linked to "personal and socially oriented activities in which they explored a range of new roles and identities" (Ivey and Broaddus 354). Finders calls this out-of-school curriculum a "literate underlife" in which students read, write, and talk about issues that are not sanctioned for them in typical classrooms (1).

One strategy to link students' out-of-school literacies with in-school comprehension and reading promotion is to modify the traditional booktalking technique. This modification, called interactive booktalking, integrates the findings of educational researchers and is more likely to accommodate the needs of today's teens.

Interactive booktalking deemphasizes the storytelling-like presentation by encouraging teens to read and discuss selected passages of books that interest them. Interactive booktalking recognizes that today's teens "live in a world vastly different from the one we and our families knew" (Bean and Readence 204). Teens face challenges and problems that teens in past decades did not. In previous times, students may have responded positively to a one-way presentation, a "talking head" approach; but today's teens need to be actively involved in the book.

There are at least four reasons for adopting an interactive booktalking approach with teens. The first reason correlates to Edwards' first booktalk objective: to sell the idea of reading for pleasure. One finding by Bodart is that teens value recommendations made in a booktalking presentation and were more likely to read these books (65). Librarians and school library media specialists who interactively booktalk are fulfilling both an important reader's advisory function but are also creating conditions for teens to become involved with the book and its characters, issues, and problems.

The second reason to adopt interactive booktalking is to meet the affective needs of teens. For some teens, their affective needs are not being met because of the dynamics of today's families which may be "ill-equipped to accommodate a child's basic, emotional, and developmental needs" (Bluestein 49). Hersch writes that many teens "spend virtually all of their discretionary time without companionship or supervision by responsible adults" (21). She asks, "How can kids imitate and learn from adults if they never talk to them?" (20). Teens benefit from opportunities to discuss the characters and situations found in young adult issues books with caring librarians and media specialists and their peers. "Most people agree, however, that normal and healthy young adults can benefit psychologically from reading and talking about the problems of fictional characters. All teenagers have problems of one type or another, and simply finding out that other people have them too provides some comfort" (Nilsen and Donelson 353).

Third, research conducted by Werner and Smith found that resilient adults had at some point in their lives had a mentor, oftentimes a teacher, who talked and listened to them and was a good role model (178). The library literature is replete with articles extolling the effectiveness of booktalking based on the number of students in the audience. This large-scale booktalking approach may have worked in the past, but students will benefit more from spending time with caring adults who connect books to their concerns, hopes, and dreams than by passively listening as books are booktalked to a large group of teens. Interactive booktalking, which emphasizes student-centered discussion, creates a much more powerful connection between books and teens than does a traditional booktalking session.

Research conducted by Gordon Wells supports the need for interactive booktalking. Wells examined the pattern of language use in home and in school during a 15-year longitudinal study. He found that in the home, children engage in conversation about as much as adults. However, in school "there was a significant imbalance in favor of teacher-talk, and therefore there were substantially fewer opportunities for students to engage in meaningful communications" (Powell 27). Too often, students are exposed to a one-sided lesson in which their opinions and beliefs are not valued. When this happens over a period of time, students may disengage from education and become apathetic (66).

Even though both traditional and interactive booktalking are often presented to an entire class, small group discussions may be extremely beneficial. Because many classes are large, teens will benefit from the personal attention of the librarian or school media specialist. Also, teens may be too self-conscious to speak in a large group. In smaller groups, teens are more likely to share their opinions, concerns, and values (Connolly and Smith 21). The discussions during interactive booktalking provide teens with opportunities to develop openmindedness and to exchange ideas.

Fourth, Edwards believed that "the best books for young adults are the books that most truly interpret to them the process of living" (Edwards 41). If Edwards were alive today, she would most likely adopt the lingo of the early 21st century to write about the importance of teens emotionally connecting with the books they are reading. Brain research recognizes the importance of the "emotional components of our memories which are critical for nearly all forms of complex learning" (Bluestein 27). This includes reading comprehension. Because teens are more actively involved during interactive booktalking, their mental processes are activated which leads to greater learning. "Movement activates our mental processes and is likewise necessary for integrating new learning into our neural circuitry" (40). Movement does not have to be active jumping and running but can be joking, talking, and responding. This fourth reason to adopt interactive booktalking correlates to the following objective communicated by Edwards: to lift the level of reading by introducing the best books the audience can read with pleasure.

The first step in interactive booktalking is selecting books that students will enjoy reading and discussing. These books can be identified in several ways: by talking with teens about their interests, problems, and concerns; by reading and learning about teen issues; and by understanding through textbooks and journal articles the types of books teens enjoy.

An interactive booktalking session generally consists of reading and discussing one book. However, within the interactive booktalking session, other books may be booktalked without being discussed. For the book that is being interactively booktalked, the librarian or school media specialist selects three to five relevant and powerful passages for group discussion.

Each student must have access to the passages being discussed. Access to the passages is important because students may need to refer to them for clarification throughout the discussion. There are several ways to ensure that each student has access to the passages. One way is to word process the passages and distribute copies to each student. A second option is to make a transparency of the passages to be shown on a wall or a screen using the overhead projector. Similar to the second option, the word processed passage can be projected on a wall or screen using a document camera or visualizer. A third option is to type the passages into a Microsoft PowerPoint™ presentation and project this onto a screen or whiteboard by using a data projector. Each of these options is satisfactory and depends on the technology available at the particular library or school.

The next step is for the librarian or school media specialist to read aloud the passages with students following along silently. Storytelling and presentation techniques may be used to draw teens further and further into the drama of the story. In addition to engaging students in the passage, reading skills are being supported which is "the only way to become good readers, develop a good writing style, and adequate vocabulary, advanced grammar, and the only way to become good spellers" (Krashen 23).

After the passage is read, the librarian or school media specialist asks students questions to encourage discussion about the book's topic, theme, characters, and issues. Students are encouraged to develop and ask their own questions. Scaffolding, which is a "set of prereading, during-reading, and post-reading opportunities and experiences designed to assist a particular group of students in successfully reading, understanding, learning from, and enjoying a particular selection," occurs during interactive booktalking (Graves and Graves 2). During the interactive booktalking session, students are encouraged to bring their own experiences to the discussion. Interactive booktalking has a strong impact on building students' literacy because of the dual interaction with the book and discussion with other students.

Interactive booktalking maintains the positive aspects of booktalking while supporting reading skills and teens' affective needs. In many ways, the purpose of interactive booktalking complements bibliotherapy which is "to foster personal insight and self-understanding among children and youth who read" (Doll and Doll 7). Appendix B contains an example of interactive booktalking.

Chapter Sixteen

Useful Web Sites for Youth Workers

The World Wide Web has a number of excellent Web sites that have information about adolescents and their issues. The following Web sites, which are categorized by issue, are recommended.

Part I: The Foundation

General Adolescent Web Sites
    The Adolescent Center
    <http://newhorizons.org>
        The Adolescent Center is devoted to the academic needs of adolescents. This Web site includes articles, links to other Web sites, and recommended reading.
    Adolescent Development Resources
    <http://www.mhhe.com/socscience/devel/teen/devel-2.htm>
        This Web site contains articles on the physical, cognitive, and social developments of adolescence plus links to student resources.
    Adolescence Directory Online
    <http://education.indiana.edu/cas/adol/adol.html>
        Adolescent Directory Online provides excellent resources for adults and teens on many adolescent issues.
    EnPsychlopedia
    <http://enpsychlopedia.com/cgi-bin/directory.cgi/Health/Mental_Health>
        This searchable mental health Web site contains almost 1,000 articles on child and adolescent issues.
    MEDLINEplus Health Information: Child and Teen Health Topics
    <http://www.nlm.nih.gov/medlineplus/childandteenhealth.html>
        Information about a variety of teen health issues, such as substance abuse, sexual health, and pregnancy, is available at the Web site.

MEDLINEplus Health Information: Teen's Page
<http://www.nlm.nih.gov/medlineplus/teenspage.html>
> This is an informative site about teens' health topics such as coping and stress, nutrition, Internet safety, homework, and how to talk to parents and other adults.

Part II: The Issues

Chapter Four: Maltreatment: Neglect and Abuse Web Sites

Mandatory Reporting of Child Abuse and Neglect
<http://www.smith-lawfirm.com/mandatory_reporting.htm>
> Attorney-at-law Susan K. Smith has developed a Web site that provides a summary of the 50 state statutes mandating persons to report child abuse and neglect.

MEDLINEplus Health Information: Child Abuse
<http://www.nlm.nih.gov/medlineplus/childabuse.html>
> This well-designed and informative Web site provides a variety of information about child and teen abuse. There are articles in Spanish.

National Clearinghouse on Child Abuse and Neglect Information
<http://www.calib.com/nccanch/>
> This extensive Web site is a national resource for professionals and provides up-to-date information about maltreatment.

Sexual Abuse of Males: Prevalence, Possible Lasting Effects, and Resources
<http://www.jimhopper.com/male-ab>
> Approximately one of every six boys is sexually abused before the age of 16. This research article provides background information about this problem.

Sexual Information and Education Council of the United States
<http://www.siecus.org/teen/teen0013.html>
> The sponsor of the Web site, SIECUS, is a national, nonprofit organization whose purpose is to educate the public about all aspects of sexuality including sexual abuse. Readers will also want to access their home page at <http://www.siecus.org>.

Chapter Five: Substance Abuse Web Sites

Drug Free AZ
<http://www.drugfreeaz.com>
> Although this Web site is produced by Arizona governmental organizations for the purpose of reducing drug use within its borders, Drug Free AZ is an information-rich resource with links to many other useful sites.

FOCUS Adolescent Services: Drugs and Teen Substance Abuse
<http://www.focusas.com/SubstanceAbuse.html>
> This site provides information about the warning signs and impact of drugs, alcohol, and tobacco on teens.

Mothers Against Drunk Driving
<http://www.madd.org>
> Established in 1980 by outraged women in California after the death of a teen by a repeat offender drunk driver, the purpose of MADD is to reduce alcohol-related fatalities.

National Institute on Drug Abuse
<http://165.112.78.61/NIDAHome.html>
> This Web site has information on many aspects of substance abuse and prevention. Links from this site are especially useful, too.

PREVLINE: Prevention Online
<http://www.health.org/>
> The goal of this searchable Web site is education and prevention of substance abuse.

Substance Abuse Theme Page
<http://www.cln.org/themes/substance_abuse.html>
> In addition to information about substance abuse, this site contains lesson plans and activities that require students to deconstruct substance abuse media messages and develop their own media presentations.

Chapter Six: Depression and Suicide Web Sites

All About Depression
<http://www.allaboutdepression.com>
> This site provides comprehensive information about clinical depression.

Andrews Depression Page
<http://www.blarg.net/~charlatn/Depression.html>
> An excellent resource about depression and suicide.

Have a Heart's Depression Resource
<http://zap.to/NoMoreShame>
> The purpose of this site is to bring awareness to the warning signs and symptoms of depression and suicide.

PsychCentral
<http://psychcentral.com>
> On Dr. Grohol's Mental Health Page, teens can be screened for a variety of mental health illnesses and problems. There are links to other mental health resources and a suicide helpline.

Teenhealth
<http://www.healthnet.com/adap/teachers/forteachers.asp>
> This Web site for teachers provides startling statistics about the prevalence of depression and suicidal thoughts. In addition, educators will learn about the symptoms of depression and what schools should do when a depressed student is identified.

Chapter Seven: Eating Disorders and Body Image Web Sites

Anorexia Nervosa and Related Eating Disorders, Inc.
<http://www.anred.com>
> This comprehensive Web site provides definitions about various eating disorders, statistics, warning signs, causes, and treatment options.

Eating Disorder Awareness and Prevention, Inc.
<http://www.nationaleatingdisorders.org>
> The Eating Disorder Awareness and Prevention site provides general information about all aspects of eating disorders.

The Media and Public Opinion
<http://members.aol.com/MrDonnLessons/Sociology.html#Media>
>Lesson plans about propaganda, advertising, and body image issues are available at this Web site.

Chapter Eight: Self-Inflicted Violence Web Sites

Healthy Place: Self-Injury Community
<http://www.healthyplace.com/Communities/Self_Injury/Site>
>A gateway to self-injury chat rooms and support groups to help teens feel less isolated is only part of what this site has to offer. In addition, there are chats on specific topics about self-injury, depression, and anxiety.

SelfHarm.com
<http://www.selfharm.com>
>The strength of this site is the links to general information about self-harm as well as personal accounts by teens that harm themselves.

Self-Injury
<http://www.self-injury.net>
>The author of this Web site is struggling with self-injury himself. This site includes links to published articles, other World Wide Web resources, and personal accounts of self-injury.

Chapter Nine: Divorce Web Sites

The Divided Heart: Helping Kids Cope with Divorce
<http://www.webheights.net/dividedheart/articles.htm>
>Articles about divorce for parents and teens, recommended books, and links to bulletin boards and newsgroups are contained on this Web site.

Divorce and Its Impact on Teens
<http://ceinfo.unh.edu/common/documents/divorce.htm>
>Sponsored by the University of New Hampshire, this is an informative article about the impact of divorce on teens.

Chapter Ten: Teen Pregnancy Web Sites

Advocates for Youth
<http://www.advocatesforyouth.org/teenpregnancy.htm>
>A wealth of resources about teen sexuality is available at this Web site. Of particular note is its "Facts" section that has a variety of statistical and numerical information about such topics as sexual abuse, pregnancy, and HIV/AIDS.

GetReal! About Teen Pregnancy
<http://www.letsgetreal.org/english/relatedsites.htm>
>This site contains links to information about teen pregnancy.

The National Campaign to Prevent Teen Pregnancy
http://www.teenpregnancy.org
>The contents of this Web site include information about pregnancy for teens, their parents, and educators.

Sexuality Information and Education Council of the United States
<http://www.siecus.org>
>SIECUS is a national, nonprofit organization that develops, collects, and dissem-

inates information about sexuality. There are links to teen sexuality resources on the World Wide Web.

Chapter Eleven: Relationship Violence Web Sites

Dating Violence
<http://www.cdc.gov/ncipc/factsheets/datviol.htm>
> This online fact sheet about dating violence was developed by the Centers for Disease Control.

Making Waves
<http://www.mwaves.org>
> Making Waves is a dating violence prevention program to help teens avoid becoming victims.

Sexual Abuse and Assault
<http://teenadvice.about.com/cs/abusesexual>
> This site offers teen advice and information about date rape for both men and women.

Teen Dating Violence
<http://www.advocatesaba.org/teens.html>
> Sponsored by Advocates Against Battering and Abuse, this Web site provides factual information about abuse and the topic of dating violence.

Chapter Twelve: Driving Web Sites

DriveHomeSafe.com
<http://www.drivehomesafe.com>
> The purpose of this Web site is to provide information and education about safe teen driving.

Driving Safety for Teenagers
<http://www.childdevelopmentinfo.com/health_safety/teen_driving.shtml>
> A variety of resources to help teens become safe drivers is available at this Web site.

Teen New Drivers' Web site
<http://www.teendriving.com/>
> This Web site is full of tips for the new teen driver on topics such as fatigue, crashes, parallel parking, buying a used car, and links to other driving information sites.

Chapter Thirteen: Bullying and Cliques Web Sites

Bully B'ware
<http://www.bullybeware.com/moreinfo.html>
> This easy-to-use Canadian Web site has information about bullies, their victims, and suggestions to stop bullying violence.

Bullying Online
<http://www.successunlimited.co.uk>
> This is one of the largest Internet resources on bullying and related issues.

Peace Building Skills
<http://members.aol.com/AngriesOut/bullyb.htm>
> This Web site provides information about conflict resolution and peace building activities.

References

Introduction

Camarena, Phame. "Self." *Adolescence in America: An Encyclopedia*. Ed. Jacqueline V. Lerner and Richard M. Lerner. 2 vols. Santa Barbara, CA: ABC CLIO. 2001.

Hersch, Patricia. *A Tribe Apart: A Journey Into the Heart of American Adolescence*. New York: Ballantine Books. 1998.

Lerner, Jacqueline V., and Richard M. Lerner. "Introduction." *Adolescence in America: An Encyclopedia*. Ed. Jacqueline V. Lerner and Richard M. Lerner. 2 vols. Santa Barbara, CA: ABC CLIO. 2001.

Werner, Emmy E., and Ruth S. Smith. *Overcoming the Odds: High Risk Children from Birth to Adulthood*. Ithica, NY: Cornell University Press. 1992

Part One: The Foundation

Chapter One: Bibliotherapy

Amer, Kim. "Using Fiction to Help Children in Two Populations Discuss Feelings." *Pediatric Nursing* 25.1 (1999): 91–6.

Bernstein, Joanne E. "Bibliotherapy: How Books Can Help Young Children Cope." *Children's Literature: Resource for the Classroom*. Ed. Masha Kabakow Rudman. Norwood: Christopher-Gordon Publishing, 1993. 159–73.

Carter, Linda Purdy. "Addressing the Needs of Reluctant Readers through Sports Literature." *The Clearing House* 71.5 (1998): 309–11.

Crothers, Samuel. "A Literary Clinic." *Atlantic Monthly 118* (1916) 291–301 qtd. in Myracle, Lauren. "Molding the Minds of the Young: The History of Bibliotherapy as Applied to Children and Adolescents." *The ALAN Review* 22 (1995): 36–40.

Doll, Beth, and Carol Doll. *Bibliotherapy with Young People: Librarians and Mental Health Professionals Working Together*. Englewood: Libraries Unlimited, Inc. 1997.

Gladding, Samuel T., and Claire Gladding. "The ABCs of Bibliotherapy for School Counselors." *School Counselor* 39 (1991): 7–13.

Gubert, Betty K. "Sadie Peterson Delaney: Pioneer Bibliotherapist." *American Libraries* 24.2 (1993): 124–9.

Kramer, Pamela A. "Using Literature to Enhance Inclusion." *Contemporary Education* 34.7 (1999): 34–7.

Lack, Clara Richardson. "Can Bibliotherapy Go Public?" *Collection Building* 7 (1985): 27–32.

Lendowsky, Barbara E., and Ronald S. Lendowsky. "Bibliotherapy for the LD Adolescent." *Academic Therapy* 14.2 (1978): 179–85.

Manning, Diane Thompson, and Bernard Manning. "Bibliotherapy for Children of Alcoholics." *Journal of Reading 27* (1984): 720–5.

Myracle, Lauren. "Molding the Minds of the Young: The History of Bibliotherapy as Applied to Children and Adolescents." *The ALAN Review 22* (1995): 36–40.

Parkeck, John T. "Using Literature to Help Adolescents Cope with Problems." *Adolescence 29.114* (1994): 421–7.

The Seven Types of Intelligences. 11 Dec. 2002
<http://www.swopnet.com/ed/TAG/7_Intelligences.html>.

Shechtman, Zipora. "An Innovative Intervention for Treatment of Child and Adolescent Aggression: An Outcome Study." *Psychology in Schools 37.2* (2000): 157–67.

Sridhar, Dheepa, and Sharon Vaughn. "Bibliotherapy for All: Enhancing Reading Comprehension, Self-Concept, and Behavior." *Teaching Exceptional Children 33.2* (2000): 74–82.

Wolpow, Ray, and Eunice N. Askov. "Strong in Broken Places: Literacy Instruction for Survivors of Pervasive Trauma." *Journal of Adolescent & Adult Literacy 42.1* (1998): 50–7.

Wolpow, Ray, and Eunice N. Askov. "Widened Frameworks and Practice: From Bibliotherapy to the Literacy of Testimony and Witness. *Journal of Adolescent & Adult Literacy 44.7* (2001): 606–9.

Chapter Two: Resiliency

Benard, Bonnie. "Fostering Resiliency in Kids." *Educational Leadership 51.3* (1993): 44–8.

Edwards, Clifford H. "Moral Classroom Communities for Student Resiliency." *The Education Digest 67.2* (2001): 15–20.

Feldman, Robert S. *Child Development.* Upper Saddle River, NJ: Prentice Hall. 1998.

Griffin, Kenneth W., et al. "Protective Role of Personal Competence Skills in Adolescent Substance Use: Psychological Well-Being as a Mediating Factor." *Psychology of Addictive Behaviors 15.3* (2001): 194–2003.

Hair, Elizabeth C., Justin Jager, and Sarah B. Garrett. *Helping Teens Develop Health Social Skills and Relationships: What the Research Shows about Navigating Adolescence.* Child Trends. 15 Oct. 2002
<http://www.childtrends.org/PDF/K3Brief.pdf>.

Hersch, Patricia. *A Tribe Apart: A Journey into the Heart of American Adolescence.* New York: Ballantine Books. 1998.

Howard, Sue, John Dryden, and Bruce Johnson. "Childhood Resilience: Review and Critique of Literature." *Oxford Review of Education 25.3* (1999): 307–23.

Katz, Mark. "Overcoming Childhood Adversities: Lessons Learned from Those Who Have 'Beat the Odds'." *Intervention in School and Clinic 32* (1997): 205–10.

Krashen, Stephen. *The Power of Reading: Insights from Research.* Englewood, CO: Libraries Unlimited, Inc. 1993.

Krovetz, Martin L. *Fostering Resiliency: Expecting All Students to Use Their Minds and Hearts Well.* Thousand Oaks, CA: Corwin Press, Inc. 1999.

Masten, Ann S. "Ordinary Magic Resilience Processes in Development." *American Psychologist 56.3* (2001): 227–38.

Welker, Eileen. *Problem Solving with Teens.* Ohio State University. 15 Oct. 2002
<http://ohioline.osu.edu/flm98/nr04.html>.

Werner, Emmy E., and Ruth S. Smith. *Overcoming the Odds: High Risk Children from Birth to Adulthood*. Ithica, NY: Cornell University Press. 1992.

Zimmerman, Marc A., Jeffrey B. Bingenheimer, and Paul C. Notaro. "Natural Mentors and Adolescent Resiliency: A Study of Urban Youth." *American Journal of Community Psychology 30.2* (2002): 221–43.

Chapter Three: Mental Health Warning Signs and Symptoms

SAMHSA. *Teen Mental Health Problems: What Are the Warning Signs. United States Department of Health and Human Services*. 2 August 2002 <http://www.mentalhealth.org/publications/allpubs/CA-0023/default.asp>

Part Two: The Issues

Chapter Four: Maltreatment

Abuse: Physical, Emotional, Sexual, Neglect. Focus Adolescent Services. 10 October 2002 <http://www.focusas.com/Abuse.html>.

Fagan, Patrick F. "The Disintegration of Family Values is Responsible for Child Abuse." *Child Abuse: Opposing Viewpoints*. San Diego: Greenhaven Press, Inc. 1999.

Henry, James, and Tom Luster. "Physical Abuse." *Adolescence in America: An Encyclopedia*. Ed. Jacqueline V. Lerner and Richard M. Lerner. 2 vols. Santa Barbara, CA: ABC CLIO. 2001.

Lowenthal, Barbara. "Effects of Maltreatment and Ways to Promote Children's Resiliency." *Childhood Education 75.4* (1999): 204–10.

Marcynyszyn, Lyscha A., and John Eckenrode. "Neglect." *Adolescence in America: An Encyclopedia*. Ed. Jacqueline V. Lerner and Richard M. Lerner. 2 vols. Santa Barbara, CA: ABC CLIO. 2001.

The National League of Cities, et al. *Ten Critical Threats to America's Children: Warning Signs for the Next Millennium*. 3 Mar. 2002 <http://www.nsba.org/highlights/ten_threats.htm>.

National Runaway Switchboard. 14 December 2002 <http://www.nrscrisisline.org>.

Perry, Bruce D. *Helping Traumatized Children: A Brief Overview for Caregivers*. 5 April 2002 <http://www.childtrauma.org/Principles2.htm>.

Physical Abuse. Focus Adolescent Services. 3 Mar. 2002 <http://www.focusas.com/Abuse.html>.

Powers, Jane Levine, and Barbara Weiss Jaklitsch. *Understanding Survivors of Abuse: Stories of Homeless and Runaway Adolescents*. Lexington, MA: Lexington Books. 1989.

Squyres, Suzanne B., Allison Landes, and Jacquelyn Quiram, ed. *Child Abuse: Betraying a Trust*. Wylie, TX: Information Plus. 1997.

Strong, Marilee. *A Bright Red Scream: Self-Mutilation and the Language of Pain*. New York: Penguin Books. 1998.

U.S. Department of Health & Human Services Administration. *Adolescent Maltreatment: Youth as Victims of Abuse and Neglect*. By Janice Hutchinson and Kristin Langlykke. 20 May 2002 <http://www.ohd.hr.state.or.us/ipe/admal.pdf>.

U.S. Department of Health & Human Services Administration. *Executive Summary of the Third National Incidence Study of Child Abuse and Neglect.* By Andrea J. Sedlak and Diane D. Broadhurst. 3 Sept. 2002 <http://www.calib.com/nccanch/pubs/statinfo/nis3.cfm>.

Wolfe, David A. et al. "Child Maltreatment:Risk of Adjustment Problems and Dating Violence in Adolescence". *Journal of the American Academy of Child and Adolescent Psychiatry 40.3* (2001): 282–9.

Zimrin, Hanita. "A Profile of Survival." *Child Abuse and Neglect 10.3* (1986): 339–50.

Chapter Five: Substance Abuse

Adair, Jan. "Tackling Teens' No. 1 Problem." *Educational Leadership 57.6* (2000): 44–7.

Alcohol and You. The High School Internet Network. 7 July 2002 <http://www.ihigh.com/0,1773,2_7_051695.00.html>.

Alcohol Use Among Teens. National Council on Alcohol and Drug Dependence. 7 July 2002 <http://www.council-houston.org/teen-alc.htm>.

American Lung Association Fact Sheet: Teen Smoking Reduced to "Not on Tobacco." 2002. American Lung Association. 12 Oct. 2002 <http://www.lungusa.org/press/tobacco/not_lead.html>.

Barrett, Joan. "Drug Abuse: Prevention Strategies for Schools." *ERIC Digest* 17.ED279644 (1986). 7 July 2002 <http://www.edu.gov/databases/ERIC_Digests/ed279644.html>.

Blum, Robert W. "Trends in Adolescent Health: Perspectives from the United States." *International Journal of Adolescent Medicine and Health 13.4* (2001): 287–295.

Blum, Robert W., and Peggy Mann Rinehart. *Reducing the Risk: Connections That Make a Difference in the Lives of Youth.* 1–40, 7 July 2002 <http://www.allaboutkids.umn.edu/cfahad/Reducing_the_risk.pdf>.

Bosworth, Kris. *Drug Abuse Prevention School-Based Strategies That Work. ERIC Digest* ED409316 (1997). 7 July 2002 <http://www.ed.gov/databases/ERIC_Digests/ed409316.html>.

Hamilton, Wendy V. *Recognizing Adolescent Alcohol Abuse: A Family Guide.* 4 September 2002 <http://www.cahe.nmsu.edu/pubs/_f/f-111.html>.

Huggins, Charnicia E. *US Teens Relate Popularity to Tobacco, Drug Use.* Reuters Health. 7 July 2002 <http://www.nlm.nih.gov/medlineplus/news/fullstory_8327.html>.

Indiana University. The Center for Adolescent Studies. "Risk Factors." *Teacher Talk 3.3* (1996). 7 July 2002 <http://education.indiana.edu/cas/tt/v3i3/riskfactors.html>.

Ladd, George T. "Substance Use and Abuse." *Adolescence in America: An Encyclopedia.* Ed. Jacqueline V. Lerner and Richard M. Lerner. 2 vols. Santa Barbara, CA: ABC CLIO, 2001.

'Let's Draw the Line' Against Underage Drinking. Mental Health Reporter. 15 February 2003 <http://www.modmh.state.mo.us/reporter/rptarc/jan_mar01/story7.html>.

Martin, Kimberly R. "Adolescent Treatment Programs Reduce Drug Abuse, Produce Other Improvements." *NIDA Notes.* 7 July 2002 <http://www.nida.nih.gov/NIDA_Notes/NNVVol17N1/Adolescent.html>.

Packer, Alex J. "Health Teachers Can Show Teens How to Get High — Without Drugs." *Curriculum Review 15* (2000). 7 July 2002 <http://www.curriculumreview.com>.

Signs of Alcohol or Drug Use. Aspen Education Group. 2 July 2002 <http://www.aspeneducation.com/factsheetsubstance.html>.

Steinberg, Laurence D. *Adolescence*. Boston: McGraw-Hill, 2002.

U.S. Department of Health and Human Services. *Monitoring the Future: National Results on Adolescent Drug Use*. By Lloyd D. Johnston, Patrick M. O'Malley, and Jerald G. Bachman. 1–61, 2002. 5 Sept. 2002 <http://monitoringthefuture.org/pubs/monographs/overview2001.pdf>.

Chapter Six: Depression and Suicide

Field, Tiffany, Miguel Diego, and Christopher Sanders. "Adolescent Depression and Risk Factors." *Adolescence 36.143* (2001): 491–8.

Gallagher, Laura A. "Suicide." *Adolescence in America: An Encylopedia*. Ed. Jacqueline V. Lerner and Richard M. Lerner. 2 vols. Santa Barbara, CA: ABC CLIO. 2001.

Health Net News. 14 December 2002 <http://www.healthnet.com/general/news/releases/dec19a.asp>.

Kenny, Maureen E. "Depression." *Adolescence in America: An Encyclopedia*. Ed. Jacqueline V. Lerner and Richard M. Lerner. 2 vols. Santa Barbara, CA: ABC CLIO. 2001.

Koplewicz, Harold S. *More Than Moody: Recognizing and Treating Adolescent Depression*. New York: G.P. Putnam's Sons. 2002.

NAMI. *Anxiety and Depression Linked to Physical Symptoms*. 13 Sept. 2002 <http://www.nami.org/youth/teendep.html>.

NAMI. *Parents of Teen Suicides Commonly Miss Depression and Other Risk Factors*. 13 Sept. 2002 <http://www.nami.org/youth/missfactor.html>.

National Mental Health Association. *Adolescent Depression: Helping Depressed Teens*. 14 Aug. 2002 <http://www.nmha.org/infoctr/factsheets/24.cfm>.

National Poll on Kids' Health and Safety. Children Now. 14 Sept. 2002 <http://www.chilrennow.org/health/HlthSftyPoll/poll_summary.html>.

Ohio's Mental Health: Building or Future Together. Mental Health and Schools. 14 Sept. 2002 <http://www.mh.state.oh.us/initiatives/forums/depression.html>.

Teenhealth. *What is Depression & What Does Depression Feel Like*. 13 Sept. 2002 <http://www.ne.healthnet.com/adap/teachers/forteachers.asp#tsigns>.

Watkins, Carol. *Child and Adolescent Depression: Diagnosis and Treatment*. 14 Aug. 2002 <http://www.baltimorepsych.com/cadepress.htm>.

Watkins, Carol. *Suicide and the School: Recognition and the Intervention for Suicidal Students in the School Setting*. 14 Aug. 2002 <http://www.baltimorepsych.com/Suicide.htm>.

Chapter Seven: Eating Disorders and Body Image

ANAD. *Facts About Eating Disorders*. National Association of Anorexia Nervosa and Associated Disorders. 15 July 2002 <http://www.anad.org/facts.htm>.

ANAD. *High School Study on Eating Disorders*. National Association of Anorexia Nervosa and Associated Disorders. 15 July 2002 <http://www.anad.org/hsstudy.htm>.

ANAD. *Warning Signs for Eating Disorders*. National Association of Anorexia Nervosa and Associated Disorders. 15 July 2002 <http://www.anad.org/warning.htm>.

Bulimia Nervosa. Eating Disorder Referral and Information Center. 15 July 2002
<http://www.edreferral.com/bulimia_nervosa.htm>.

"Certain Behaviors Can Predict Binge-Eating Disorders in Teenage Girls." *Ascribe Higher Education News Service* 14 Mar. 2002: NA. Info Trac. Nova Southeastern Univ. Lib., Ft. Lauderdale, FL. 30 Jan. 2003. <http://www.novaedu/library>.

Chaves, Anne. "Eating Problems." *Adolescence in America: An Encyclopedia*. Ed. Jacqueline V. Lerner and Richard M. Lerner. 2 vols. Santa Barbara, CA: ABC CLIO. 2001.

National Eating Disorders Association. *Anorexia Nervosa*. 15 July 2002 <http://www.nationaleatingdisorders.org>.

National Eating Disorders Association. *Prevention Guidelines & Strategies*. 15 July 2002 <http://www.nationaleatingdisorders.org>.

Pipher, Mary. *Reviving Ophelia: Saving the Selves of Adolescent Girls*. New York: The Ballantine Group. 1994.

Pruitt, David B. *Your Adolescent: Emotional, Behavioral, and Cognitive Development*. New York: HarperResource. 1999.

Rothenberg, Dianne. "Supporting Girls in Early Adolescence." *ERIC Digest* ED386331 (1995). 15 Sept. 2002 <http://www.edu/gov/databases/ERIC_Digests/ed386331.html>.

Thomsen, Steven R., Michelle W. Weber, and Lora Beth Brown. "The Relationship Between Reading Beauty and Fashion Magazines and the Use of Pathogenic Dieting Methods Among Adolescent Females." *Adolescence 37* (2002): 1–18.

"Timing of Menarch and Eating Disorder Symptoms." *Nutrition Research Newsletter 21.3* (2002): 10.

YM: Diet Stories No More.
<http://www.wnyc.org/onthemedia/transcripts_012602_ym.html>

Chapter Eight: Self-Inflicted Violence

AAMFT. *Adolescent Self-Harm*. American Association for Marriage and Family Therapy. 16 Apr. 2002 <http://www.aamft.org/families/Consumer_Updates/Adolescent_Self-Harm.htm>

Alderman, Tracy. *The Scarred Soul: Understanding & Ending Self-Inflicted Violence*. Oakland, CA: New Harbinger Publications, Inc. 1997.

Gallagher, Laura A. "Self-Injury." *Adolescence in America: An Encyclopedia*. Ed. Jacqueline V. Lerner and Richard M. Lerner. 2 vols. Santa Barbara, CA: ABC CLIO. 2001.

Holmes, Ann. *Cutting Away the Pain: Understanding Self-Mutilation*. Philadelphia: Chelsea House Publications. 2000.

Morton, Andrew. *Diana: Her True Story*. New York: Simon and Schuster. 1993.

Ng, Gina. *Self-Mutilation: A Helping Book for Teens Who Hurt Themselves*. New York: The Rosen Publishing Group, Inc. 1998.

Strong, Merilee. *A Bright Red Scream: Self-Mutilation and the Language of Pain*. New York: Penguin Putnam. 1998.

Chapter Nine: Divorce

Adolescence: Change and Continuity. 19 July 2002
<http://www.personal.psu.edu/faculty/n/x/nxd10/adfamb2.htm>.

Adolescents and Divorce. 19 July 2002
<http://www.divorceinfo.com/chadolescents.htm>.

Blum, Robert W. *Reducing the Risk: Connections That Make a Difference in the Lives of Youth*. 19 July 2002
<http://www.allaboutkids.umn.edu/cfahad/Reducing_the_risk.pdf>.

Divorce and Its Impact on Teens. University of New Hampshire Cooperative Extension. 19 July 2002 <http://www.ceinfo.unh.edu/common/documents/divorce.htm>.

Haggerty, Robert J., et al. *Stress, Risk, and Resilience in Children and Adolescents: Processes, Mechanisms, and Interventions*. Cambridge: Cambridge University Press. 1996.

Miller, Paul A., Patti Ryan, and William Morrison. "Practical Strategies for Helping Children of Divorce in Today's Classroom." *Childhood Education* 75.5 (1999): 285–9.

Rodriguez, Hilda, and Chandler Arnold. *Children and Divorce: A Snapshot*. Oct. 1998. Center for Law and Social Policy. 19 July 2002
<http://www.clasp.org/pubs/familyformation/divfinal.htm>.

Wallerstein, Judith, Julia M. Lewis, and Sandra Blakeslee. *Unexpected Legacy of Divorce: A 25 Year Landmark Study*. New York: Hyperion. 2000.

Wong, Mai-Lon. "At-Risk? Building the Cords of Resiliency." *American Secondary Education* 25.97 (2000): 1–7.

Chapter Ten: Teen Pregnancy

CDC. *U.S. Pregnancy Rate Lowest in Two Decades*. Centers for Disease Control and Prevention. 20 Aug. 2002
<http://www.cdc.gov/nchs/releases/00facts/trends.htm>.

"Curricular Programs to Curb Teen Pregnancy." *The Education Digest* 64.7 (1999): 38–41.

Davies, Linda, Margaret McKinnon, and Prue Rains. "Creating a Family: Perspectives from Teen Mothers." *Journal of Progressive Human Services* 12.1 (2001): 83–100.

East, Patricia L., and Marianne E. Felice. *Adolescent Parenting: Findings from a Racially Diverse Sample*. Mahwah, NJ: Earlbaum. 1996.

Hanson, Sandra, David E. Myers, and Alan L. Ginsberg. "The Role of Responsibility and Knowledge in Reducing Teenage Out-of-Wedlock Childbearing." *Journal of Marriage and the Family* 49 (1987): 241–56.

Kivisto, Peter. "Teenagers, Pregnancy, and Childbearing in a Risk Society." *Journal of Family Issues* 22.8 (2001): 1044–65.

Lewis, Susan K., Catherine E. Ross, and John Mirowsky. "Establishing a Sense of Personal Control in the Transition to Adulthood." *Social Forces* 77.4 (1999): 1573–99.

Martin, Joyce A., Brady E. Hamilton, and Stephanie J. Ventura. National Vital Statistics. Centers for Disease Control and Prevention. 20 Sept. 2002
<http://www.cdc.gov/nchs/data/nvsr/nvsr49/nvsr49_05.pdf>.

The National Campaign to Prevent Teen Pregnancy. *Partners in Progress: The Education Community and Preventing Teen Pregnancy.* 20 July 2002 <http://www.teenpregnancy.org/resources/reading/pdf/partnersprogress.pdf>.

Nitz, Katherine. "Pregnancy, Interventions to Prevent." *Adolescence in America: An Encyclopedia.* Ed. Jacqueline V. Lerner and Richard M. Lerner. 2 vols. Santa Barbara. CA: ABC CLIO. 2001.

Pruitt, David B. *Your Adolescent: Emotional, Behavioral, and Cognitive Development from Early Adolescence through the Teen Years.* New York: HarperResource. 1999.

Resnick, Michael, Peter Bearman, and Robert Blum. "Protecting Adolescents from Harm: Findings from the National Longitudinal Study on Adolescent Health." *Journal of the American Medical Association 287.10* (1997): 823–832.

Zimmerman, Rick S., et al. "Adolescents' Perceived Ability to Say 'No' to Unwanted Sex." *Journal of Adolescent Research 10* (1995): 383–399.

Chapter Eleven: Relationship Violence

Advocates for Youth. *Dating Violence Among Adolescents.* Mar. 2000. 29 July 2002 <http://www.advocatesforyouth.org/publicatons/factsheet/fsdating.htm>.

Curtis, David G. *Perspectives on Acquaintance Rape.* 29 June 2002 <http://aaetx.org/arts/art13.htm>.

Gedatus, Guy. *Date and Acquaintance Rape.* Mankato, MN: Capstone Press, 2000.

James, William H., et al. "Youth Dating Violence." *Adolescence 35.139* (2000): 455–65.

Lindquist, Scott. *The Date Rape Prevention Book: The Essential Guide for Girls & Women.* Naperville, IL: Sourcebooks, Inc. 2000.

Warshaw, Robin. *I Never Called it Rape: The Ms. Report on Recognizing, Fighting and Surviving Date and Acquaintance Rape.* New York: HarperPerennial. 1994.

What You Need to Know About Dating Violence. Liz Claiborne Inc. 3 Feb. 2003 <http://www.lizclaiborne.com/lizinc/lizworks/women/pdf/teen_handbook.pdf>.

Wolfe, David A., et al. "Child Maltreatment: Risk of Adjustment Problems and Dating Violence in Adolescence." *Journal of the American Academy of Child and Adolescent Psychiatry 40.3* (2001): 282–9.

Zimmerman, Rick S., et al. "Adolescents' Perceived Ability to Say 'No' to Unwanted Sex." *Journal of Adolescent Research 10.3* (1995): 383–99.

Chapter Twelve: Driving

AmISafe? *Let's Get Serious.* 2001. 4 June 2002 <http://www.amisafe.net>.

Dewan, Sheila K. "Albany Votes to Suspend Licenses of Teenagers Caught Driving Drunk." *The New York Times.* 23 Apr. 2002: B5.

DriveHomeSafe.com. *Teen Driving Information and Stuff for New Teen Drivers.* 2000. 3 June 2002 <http://www.drivehomesafe.com/just_4_teens.htm>.

MADD. *Stats & Resources.* Mothers Against Drunk Driving. 4 June 2002 <http://www.madd.org/stats/0,1056,1807,00.html>.

NHTSA. *Traffic Safety Facts 2000.* National Highway Traffic Safety Administration. 4 June 2002 < http://www-fars.nhtsa.dot.gov/pubs/15.pdf >.

Ponton, Lynn E. *The Romance of Risk.* New York: Basic Books. 1997.

Rumbach, David. "Time to Mature: New Research Suggest Teens' Risky Behaviors, such as Drinking and Driving, may Be an 'Outgrowth of their Brains'." *South Bend Tribune*. 22 Apr. 2002: N/A.

Runyan, Carol W., and Elizabeth A. Gerken. "Epidemiology and Prevention of Adolescent Injury: A review and Research Agenda." *The Journal of the American Medical Association 262.16* (1989): 2273–80.

"The Teenage Driver." *Pediatrics 98.5* (1996): 987–91.

Chapter Thirteen: Bullying and Cliques

Garbarino, James, and Ellen deLara. *And Words Can Hurt Forever: How to Protect Adolescents from Bullying, Harassment, and Emotional Violence*. New York: The Free Press. 2002.

Huebner, Angela, and Erin Morgan. *Adolescent Bullying*. Apr. 2002. Virginia Cooperative Extension. 6 May 2002 <http://www.ext.vt.edu/pubs/family/350-852/350-852.html>.

Krovetz, Martin L. *Fostering Resiliency: Expecting All Students to Use Their Minds and Hearts Well*. Thousand Oaks, CA: Corwin Press, Inc. 1999.

Middleton-Moz, Jan, and Mary Lee Zawadski. *Bullies: From the Playground to the Boardroom*. Deerfield Beach, FL: Health Communications, 2002.

More Information on Bullying. Bully B'Ware Productions. 6 May 2002 <http://www.bullybeware.com/moreinfo.html>.

Nansel, Tonja R., et al. "Bullying Behaviors among US Youth." *Journal of the American Medical Association 285.16* (2001): 2094–2100.

Olson, Laura Hess. "Bullying." *Adolescence in America: An Encyclopedia*. Ed. Jacqueline V. Lerner and Richard M. Lerner. 2 vols. Santa Barbara, CA: ABC CLIO. 2001.

Pollock, William. *Real Boys' Voices*. New York: Random House. 2000.

Simmons, Rachel. *Odd Girl Out*. New York: Harcourt. 2002.

Watkins, Carol E. *Dealing with Bullies and How Not to Be One*. 2000. Northern County, MD, Psychiatric Associates. 6 May 2002 <http://www.ncpamd.com/Bullies.htm>.

Weinhold, Barry K. *Bullying and School Violence: The Tip of the Iceberg*. 6 May 2002 <http://ericcass.uncg.edu/virtuallib/bullying/1059.html>.

Part Three: Bringing Attention to the Issues

Chapter Fourteen: Calendar of Events

Krovetz, Martin L. *Fostering Resiliency: Expecting All Students to Use Their Minds and Hearts Well*. Thousand Oaks, CA: Corwin Press, Inc. 1999.

Chapter Fifteen: Interactive Booktalking

Bean, Thomas W., and John E. Readence. "Adolescent Literacy: Charting a Course for Successful Futures as Lifelong Learners." *Reading Research and Instruction 41.3* (2002): 203–210.

Bluestein, Jane. *Creating Emotionally Safe Schools: A Guide for Educators and Parents*.

Deerfield Beach, FL: Health Communications, Inc., 2001.

Bodart, Joni. *The Effect of a Booktalk Presentation of Selected Titles on the Attitude Toward Reading of Senior High School Students and of the Circulation of These Titles in the High School Library*. Diss. Texas Women's University, 1987. Ann Arbor, MI: UMI, 1987. 8729673.

Chelton, Mary Kay. "Booktalking—You Can Do It." *School Library Journal 22* (1976): 39–42.

Connolly, Bill and Michael W. Smith. "Teachers and Students Talk About Talk: Class Discussion and the Way It Should Be." *Journal of Adolescent & Adult Literacy 46.1* (2002): 16–26.

Doll, Beth, and Carol Doll. *Bibliotherapy with Young People: Librarians and Mental Health Professionals Working Together*. Englewood, CO: Libraries Unlimited, Inc. 1997.

Edwards, Margaret A. *The Fair Garden and the Swarm of Beasts: The Library and the Young Adult*. New York: Hawthorn Books, Inc. 1974.

Finders, Margaret J. *Just Girls: Hidden Literacies and Life in Junior High*. Urbana: IL: National Council of Teachers of English and New York: Teachers College Press. 1999.

Graves, Michael, and Bonnie Graves. *Scaffolding Reading Experience*. Norwood, MA: Christopher-Gordon. 1994.

Hersch, Patricia. *A Tribe Apart: A Journey into the Heart of American Adolescence*. New York: Ballantine Books. 1998.

Ivey, Gay, and Karen Broaddus. "Just Plain Reading: A Survey of What makes Students Want to Read in Middle School Classrooms." *Reading Research Quarterly 36.4* (2001): 350–377.

Krashen, Stephen. *The Power of Reading: Insights from Research*. Englewood, CO: Libraries Unlimited, Inc. 1993.

Nilsen, Alleen Pace, and Kenneth L. Donelson. *Literature for Today's Young Adults*. 6th ed. New York: Longman. 2001.

Powell, Rebecca. *Literacy as a Moral Imperative*. Lanham, MD: Rowman & Littlefield Publishers, Inc. 1999.

Reeder, Gail M. *Effect of Booktalks on Adolescent Reading Attitudes*. Diss. University of Nebraska. 1991. Ann Arbor, MI: UMI Dissertation Services. 1991. 9129570.

Werner, Emmy E., and Ruth S. Smith. *Overcoming the Odds: High Risk Children from Birth to Adulthood*. Ithica, NY: Cornell University Press. 1992.

Appendix B: Interactive Booktalking of Driver's Ed by Carolyn B. Cooney

Bloom's Taxonomy. 12 Oct. 2002
<http://www.coun/uvic.ca/learn/program/hndouts/bloom.html>.

Chapter 4: Bloom's Taxonomy. Distance Learning Resource Network. 12 Oct. 2002
<http://www.dlrn.org/library/dl/guide4.html>.

Cooney, Caroline B. *Driver's Ed*. New York: Bantam Doubleday Dell Books for Young Readers. 1994.

Huitt, William. *Critical Thinking*. 12 Oct. 2002
<http://chiron.valdosta.edu/whuitt/col/cogsys/critthnk.hmtl>.

Appendix A

"Must Reads" for Youth Workers

The following books about adolescents are recommended for the librarian, media specialist, or other youth worker.

Adolescence in America: An Encyclopedia. **eds. Jacqueline V. Lerner and Richard M. Lerner. 2 vols. Santa Barbara, CA: ABC CLIO. 2001.**
Brief but highly informative articles on a variety of teen topics from abortion to youth outlook are contained in this two volume encyclopedia. Adults and teens will find this encyclopedia to be a good starting place when looking for information on teen issues.

Blaustein, Jane. ***Creating Emotionally Safe Schools: A Guide for Educators and Parents.*** **Deerfield Beach, FL: Health Communications, Inc. 2001.**
The author provides evidence that quality education consists of schools that are emotionally safe and academically sound. This book is a valuable addition to the school safety literature.

Garbarino, James and Ellen deLara. ***And Words Can Hurt Forever: How to Protect Adolescents from Bullying, Harassment, and Emotional Violence.*** **New York: The Free Press. 2002.**
Garbarino and deLara bring attention to the overall destructiveness of bullying and communicate to the reader that if bullying is to end, it is the responsibility of adults. School safety must be assured by adults who recognize that violence exists and develop the requisite interventions and programs.

Hersch, Patricia. ***A Tribe Apart: A Journey into the Heart of American Adolescence.*** **New York: Ballantine Books. 1998.**
After reading this book, adults will never look at teens in quite the same way. In this absolute must read, Hersch shadowed a group of teens for one year to learn about their secret lives, the pressures they face, and what school is really like. What she found is heart-breaking and will forever change the way one deals with teens.

Koplewicz, Harold S. ***More Than Moody: Recognizing and Treating Adolescent Depression.*** **New York: G.P. Putnam's Sons. 2002.**
This very thorough book was written to help parents and educators understand and recognize the difference between teenage moodiness and the depression that affects nearly 3.5 million children and teenagers in the United States.

Pipher, Mary. ***Reviving Ophelia: Saving the Selves of Adolescent Girls.*** **New York: Ballantine Books. 1994.**
In this ground-breaking book that was published almost a decade ago, Pipher brings attention to the special needs of adolescent girls. According to Pipher, teen girls are experiencing an extraordinary amount of pressure and negativity as a result of living in a "girl-poisoning culture" (12). A revised edition with an updated foreword has been published.

Pollack, William S. *Real Boys' Voices.* **New York: Random House. 2000.**
>Pollack, a clinical psychologist and assistant clinical professor of psychiatry at Harvard Medical School, has written a very readable book that will help parents and teachers understand the pressures facing adolescent boys. Pollack and his research team traveled around the country and interviewed boys about a myriad of topics such as gender roles, sex, the pressure to succeed, depression, bullying, relationship with parents, friendship and romance, substance abuse, and the effects of divorce.

Ponton, Lynn E. *The Romance of Risk: Why Teenagers Do the Things They Do.* **New York: Basis Books-Perseus Books Group. 1997.**
>If you have ever wondered why teens take the risks that they do, then Ponton's book will help you understand. Ponton asserts that teens' natural inclination to take risks whether with drugs, driving, or unprotected sex can be redirected into healthy channels.

Ponton, Lynn E. *The Sex Lives of Teenagers: Revealing the Secret World of Adolescent Boys and Girls.* **New York: Dutton. 2000.**
>Ponton, a psychotherapist, has written an informative book about one of the greatest taboo subjects in our culture—sex. Ponton addresses pregnancy, abortion, masturbation, sexual orientation, Internet dating, and gender roles.

Simmons, Rachel. *Odd Girl Out: The Hidden Culture of Aggression in Girls.* **New York: Harcourt. 2002.**
>Girls bully differently from boys—theirs is aimed at shunning, dropping friends without any reason, and spreading rumors. By interviewing teen girls, Simmons uncovers the dynamics of relational aggression and brings attention to the pain, the anger, and the danger of this form of violence.

Strong, Mariliee. *A Bright Red Scream: Self-Mutilation and the Language of Pain.* **New York: Penguin Books. 1998.**
>Strong, an award-winning journalist, has produced a book that is a must read on the topic of self-harm and abuse. She eloquently communicates the pain of self-harm and why teens hurt themselves.

Appendix B

Interactive Booktalking of *Driver's Ed* by Caroline B. Cooney

The purposes of interactive booktalking are to promote and establish reading as a lifelong habit, provide students with an opportunity to make connections between books and their lives, and improve reading skills. Interactive booktalking also develops critical thinking which is the "disciplined mental activity of evaluating arguments of propositions and making judgments that can guide the development of beliefs and taking action" (Huitt, par. 2).

Interactive booktalking begins with the librarian or school media specialist selecting passages from a book which has strong teen appeal. The passages should be meaningful to teens so that they can identify and easily discuss similarities or dissimilarities between their life experiences and those of characters in the story. Secondarily, the passages are selected and discussed for the purpose of developing skills in reading, comprehension, vocabulary, inference, prediction, and decision making.

In the 1940s and 1950s, Benjamin Bloom headed a group of educational psychologists to develop a "classification of levels of intellectual behavior important in learning" (*Chapter 4*, par. 1). The resulting book, *Bloom's Taxonomy of the Cognitive Domain*, categorizes the six hierarchies of student learning. These hierarchies are levels of abstraction of questions that commonly occur in educational settings (pars. 1–7). The six categories range from the lowest level of abstraction, simple recall, to the highest order, evaluation. The six levels of intellectual activity are: knowledge, comprehension, application, analysis, synthesis, and evaluation (*Chapter 4*, par. 3). Following the questions in the *Driver's Ed* interactive booktalking, the level of questioning is identified in parentheses.

For each interactive booktalk, questions should be developed that reflect each level of intellectual activity. In this way, students will have the opportunity to both recall incidents from the book, but also to consider and discuss the book in terms of their own life experiences, decision-making, and development of critical-thinking skills.

The following is an example of an interactive booktalk of *Driver's Ed* which was used with high school students who are English second language learners. Four passages were selected for discussion. The story is about teens who decide it would be an exciting prank to take street signs. However, when a stop sign is taken which leads to the death of 26-year-old Denise Thompson, the teens struggle with their participation in the prank. The bibliographic information for this book is: Cooney, Caroline B. *Driver's Ed*. New York: Bantam Doubleday Dell Books for Young Readers. 1994. ISBN: 0-440-21981-7.

In the first passage in Chapter Two on page 23 in this edition, Lark, a popular student in the driver education class, responds to the recent spate of mailbox vandalism by suggesting her fellow students take signs. The passage begins with "*Lots of idiots go out...*" and ends with "*Let's make it a class game.*"

Questions for Passage One:

1. What class are these students taking? (Knowledge)
2. Explain why Lark suggests taking signs. (Comprehension)
3. As a group, brainstorm the consequences of sign taking. (Analysis)
4. If you had been in this class, would you have participated in the sign taking? Why or why not? (Synthesis)
5. Have you ever taken signs? What led you to take signs? (Analysis)
6. Carefully reread the first sentence. What could have happened previously in the story to make painting initials on rocks, painting bridges, or smashing mailboxes worth mentioning? (Evaluate)
7. Lark pronounces that students should "take signs." Instead of "take," identify other words that Lark could have used. (Synthesis)
8. What words or actions could have made the students decide not to take signs? (Analysis)

In the second passage in Chapter Three on pages 51–52 in this edition, Nickie, Morgan, and Remy have been cutting down street signs for about two hours. It is now 9:45 p.m. They are parked near the busy intersection of Cherry Road and Warren Street and are about to cut down the most desirable sign of all—a stop sign. The passage begins with "*Nickie stopped a mile from...*" and ends with "*Nickie turned on the engine, flicked the headlights up, and took off.*"

Questions for Passage Two:

1. In your own words, restate what is happening in this passage. (Knowledge)
2. Name the teens involved in this incident. (Knowledge)
3. What is the relationship between Remy and Morgan? Refer to the passage to find clues about their relationship. (Comprehension)
4. Do you think that Remy and Morgan were influenced by each other to take signs because they were becoming a couple? Or less likely? (Analysis)
5. Has there ever been a time that you were talked into doing something you did not want to do? Explain. (Synthesis)
6. Which street did the teens park on? (Knowledge)
7. Describe Cherry Road. Describe Warren Street. (Knowledge)
8. Reread the passage to find clues about Nicki. How would you describe Nicki? Would parents like Nicki? (Comprehension)
9. So far, which signs have been cut down? (Knowledge)
10. As a result of cutting down these signs, predict what will happen next. (Comprehension)

In the third passage in Chapter Four on pages 67–69 in this edition, Anne, an anchor on the local nightly news, announces the death of Mrs. Thompson as a result of the previous night's sign taking. On her way home after dropping off the babysitter, Mrs. Thompson is hit broadside by a truck. She dies instantly. A policeman at the scene of the crash blames *"Kids…They don't think. They like the shape of stop signs, you know."* The passage begins with *"And now, a spate of…"* and ends with *"This Denise Thompson, she's a stranger to the roads, she needs that stop sign."*

Questions for Passage Three:

1. What emotions is Morgan experiencing as he watches the news announcement about Mrs. Thompson's death? Have you ever felt these emotions? Describe the incident that caused you to experience these emotions. (Knowledge/Comprehension)
2. Who is Anne? (Knowledge)
3. "Last night a fatal car accident occurred at the corner of Warren Street and Cherry Road." Look up the word "accident" in the dictionary. What is the definition of accident? Was Mrs. Thompson's death an accident? Can you think of other words that are more appropriate? (Synthesis)
4. Reread the beginning of the passage. Why are there no quotes around the words sign stealing? (Analysis)
5. Why does the policeman think kids took the stop sign? Point to evidence in the passage that supports the policeman's assertion that kids took the stop sign. (Application)
6. Have you ever been blamed for doing something that you did not do? If yes, why do you think you were blamed? (Analysis)
7. Do you think that teens are blamed unjustly for things they did not do? (Analysis)
8. Why do kids take signs? Brainstorm strategies to stop sign taking among teens. (Evaluate)
9. If you were the police chief and you were convinced that teens had taken this sign, what would you do? (Analysis)
10. What other actions and behaviors are teens involved in that are potentially harmful or life-threatening to them or others? Why do teens do these things? (Evaluation)

In the fourth passage in Chapter Six on page 102 in this edition, Morgan and Remy's shame and guilt grows as they read the advertisement Mrs. Thompson's distraught husband places in the local newspaper. It is a reward for information about the killer—the murderer—of his wife. The passage begins with *"Who murdered my wife?"* and ends with *"Tell me who murdered my wife."*

Questions for Passage Four:

1. Who is responsible for placing this announcement in the newspaper? (Knowledge)

2. What do you think Mr. Thompson is hoping to gain from running this announcement in the paper? (Analysis)
3. If someone you love was killed as a result of a stolen sign, what actions would you take? (Synthesis)
4. Pretend you are one of the teens. Describe the emotions you are feeling. (Evaluate)
5. After reflecting on what has been read so far, what do you think will happen next? (Synthesis)
6. What is the moral of *Driver's Ed*? What did you learn? (Application)
7. Pretend that there has been a sign stealing incident at your school which has resulted in death. The principal wants to develop a program to educate teens about the dangers of sign stealing. You have been asked to be on the committee to develop this program. What would be your suggestions for this program? (Synthesis)

Depending on the number and complexity of the questions and the amount of discussion, an interactive booktalk presentation can take anywhere from 15 minutes to one hour. As librarians and school library media specialists are reading books to determine whether they should be interactively booktalked, it is helpful to identify sentences and paragraphs that might be appropriate for discussion. Once the first reading of the book has been completed, librarians and school library media specialists can refer to their lists of passages to determine those that encourage maximum discussion and meet the objectives of the interactive booktalk.

As stated earlier in this appendix, within the interactive booktalk it is beneficial to ask questions that fall into each category of *Bloom's Taxonomy*. In this way, students will have the opportunity to recall incidents from the book as well as to discuss the story in light of their experiences, make good decisions, and develop critical-thinking skills.

Index

1993 Third National Incidence Study of Child Abuse and Neglect 18

A

Abuse. 20–22
    characteristics. 20, 22
    comparisons 22
    emotional 21
    manifestation of problems 22
    physical 20
    sexual. 20
Adolescence vii
    transition to middle school 38
After the Death of Anna Gonzales (Fields) 40
Aimee (Miller) 42
Alderman, Tracy. *The Scarred Soul* 52, 53
Anderson, Laurie Halse. *Speak*. 76
Anonymous. *Go Ask Alice* 33
Anorexia Nervosa. 45–47
    characteristics. 45
    definition 46
    depression 46
    warning signs 46–47, 59
Awareness days
    Dr. Martin Luther King, Jr. Commemorative Holiday. 93
    International Literacy Day 97
    Juneteenth 95
    Lights on After School 98
    National Childhood Depression Day. 96
    National Day to Prevent Teen Pregnancy, The. . . . 96
    National Depression Screening Day 98
    National Peer Helpers Day 98
    National Self-Injury Awareness Day 94
    Turn Beauty Inside Out Day 96
    World AIDs Day. 99
Awareness months
    Alcohol Awareness Month 95
    Attention Deficit Disorder Month. 99
    Black History Month 94
    Child Abuse Prevention Month. 95
    Domestic Violence Awareness Month 98
    Gay and Lesbian Month 97
    Haitian Heritage Month 95
    Hispanic Heritage Month 97
    Mental Health Month 96
    Month of the Young Adolescent 98
    National Alcohol and Drug Recovery Month 97
    National American Indian Heritage Month 99
    National Asian Pacific Heritage Month 96
    National Bike Month 96
    National Disability Employment Awareness Month. 98
    National Drunk and Drugged Driving Prevention Month 99
    National Hobby Month. 94
    National Library Card Sign-up Month 97
    National Mentoring Month. 94
    National Native American Awareness Month 99
    National Poetry Month 95
    National Runaway Prevention Month 99
    National Women's History Month. 95
Awareness weeks
    Buckle Up America 96
    National Eating Disorders Awareness Week 94
    National Mental Illness Awareness Week 98
    National Suicide Awareness Week 96
    Random Acts of Kindness Week. 94
    Red Ribbon Week. 98
    You Drink & Drive. You Lose 97

B

Backwater (Bauer) 13
Bauer, Joan
    Backwater 13
    "Extra Virgin" in *Love & Sex: Ten Stories of Truth* (Cart). 69
Beauty Queen (Glovach) 34
Bechard, Margaret. *Hanging on to Max* 68
Benard, Bonnie 7
Bibliotherapy 1–5
    consistent with education 3
    controversy. 1–2
    Delaney, Sadie Peterson 1
    first usage 2
    identification, catharsis, and insight 1
    multiple intelligences 4
    purposes of. 2
    technology 4–5
    types of 2
    with special needs youth. 3
Bibliotherapy with Young People: Librarians and Mental Health Professionals Working Together (Doll and Doll) vii
Black-eyed Suzie (Shaw) 24
Blaustein, Jane. *Creating Emotionally Safe Schools: A Guide for Educators and Parents*. 122
Bloom, Benjamin 124
Bloom's Taxonomy of the Cognitive Domain 124
Bloor, Edward. *Tangerine*. 88
Bodart, Joni 101
Body of Christopher Creed, The (Plum-Ucci) 91
Books, healing powers of 1
Booktalking 101–105

    interactive 102–105, 124–127
    objectives 101
    techniques 101–102
Booktalking dissertations
    Bodart, Joni 101
    Reeder, Gail M. 101
Borderlands (Dewey) 41
Born Blue (Nolan) 26
Borrowed Light (Fienberg) 69
Breaking Point (Flinn) 90
Breathing Underwater (Flinn) 77
Buchanan, Jane. *Hank's Story*. 22
Bulimia Nervosa 45, 47
    Definition of 47
    Prevention of 47–48
Bulimics, characteristics of 47
Bullying 85–88
    behavior 85
    by boys 86
    by girls 86
    consequences of 86
    prevention by educators 87–88
    relational aggression 86
    targets of 87
Bullying study
    National Institute of Child Health and Human
        Development 86
Burgess, Melvin
    Junk 33
    Smack 33
Burnett, Cheryl. *Life in the Fat Lane* 49

C

Cart, Michael. *Love & Sex: Ten Stories of Truth* 69
Caseley, Judith. *Losing Louisa* 62
Catharsis 1–2
Charlie's Run (Hobbs) 60
Cohn, Rachel. *Gingerbread* 62
Cole, Brock. *The Facts Speak for Themselves* 25
Conly, Jane Leslie. *What Happened on Planet Kid* 23
Conquering the Beast Within: How I Fought
    Depression and Won...And How You
    Can, Too (Irwin) 41
Cooney, Caroline
    Driver's Ed 81
    Driver's Ed Interactive Booktalking 124
    Tune in Anytime (Cooney) 63
Corrigan, Eireann. *You Remind Me of You:*
    A Poetry Memoir 49
Couloumbis, Audrey. *Say Yes* 11
Creating Emotionally Safe Schools: A Guide
    for Educators and Parents (Blaustein) 122
Cruise, Robin. *The Top-Secret Journal of Fiona*
    Claire Jardin 60
Crutcher, Chris
    "Guns for Geeks" in *On the Fringe* (Gallo) 91
    Staying Fat for Sarah Byrnes 25
    Whale Talk 91
Cut (McCormick) 55

Cutters
    See Self-inflicted violence

D

A Dance for Three (Plummer) 70
Dancing Naked (Hrdlitschka) 69
Date rape 74–76
    acquaintances 75
    definition of 74
    effects of 75
    not reported 74–75
    planned attack 75
    prevention 76
Date rape drugs
    Gamma Hydoxybutrate 75
    Rohypnol 75
Deans, Sis. *Racing the Past* 88
Death at Devil's Bridge (DeFelice) 32
Deaver, Julie Reece. *The Night I Disappeared* 25
Decision-making skills 4, 10
    See also Resiliency
DeFelice, Cynthia. *Death at Devil's Bridge* 32
Delaney, Sadie Peterson 1
Depression 17, 37–40
    divorce 59
    differences between adults and youth 38
    genetic predisposition 38
    symptoms among teens 37–38
    treatment 39
Dessen, Sarah
    Dreamland 77
    Keeping the Moon 13
    Someone Like You 69
    That Summer 63
    This Lullaby 63
Dewey, Jennifer Owings. *Borderlands* 41
Diet 46
Divorce 57–60
    advice to educators 59
    conflict 58
    financial impact of 57
    initial stage of 58
    longitudinal study 58
    negative consequences of 57, 59
    reaction of teen boys to 59
    reaction of teen girls to 59
    statistics 57
Doll, Beth and Carol
    Bibliotherapy with Young People: Librarians
        and Mental Health Professionals Working
        Together vii
    purposes of bibliotherapy 2
Don't Think Twice (Pennebaker) 70
Don't You Dare Read This, Mrs. Dunphrey (Haddix) . . . 26
Door Near Here, A (Quarles) 27
Double Dutch (Draper) 12
Draper, Sharon
    Double Dutch 12
    Tears of a Tiger 41, 81

Drawing Lessons (Mack) 61
Dreamland (Dessen) 77
Dream Where the Losers Go, The (Goobie) 55
Driver's Ed (Cooney)....................... 81
    interactive booktalking 124
Driving........................... 79–80
    and drinking 80
    factors contributing to crashes 79–80
    graduated license laws 80
    prevention of crashes 80
    rate of crashes 79
    teens' brain 80
Drug use
    See Substance use and abuse
Duncan, Lois
    I Know What You Did Last Summer 81
    On the Edge: Stories at the Brink 26, 56

E

Eating disorders 45–48
    body image.......................... 46
    counteracting media messages 48
    Seventeen 46
    statistics 45
    Teen 46
    YM 46
    See also Anorexia Nervosa
    See also Bulimia Nervosa
Educational neglect
    See Neglect, educational
Edwards, Margaret A. 101
Emotional neglect
    See Neglect, emotional
Emotional or psychological abuse
    See Maltreatment
    See Abuse, emotional
Endorphins 53
"Extra Virgin" (Bauer) in Love & Sex:
    Ten Stories of Truth Cart) 69
External assets
    See Resiliency

F

Facts Speak for Themselves, The (Cole) 25
Fat Chance (Newman)...................... 48
Feather Boy (Singer) 90
Ferris, Amy Schor. A Greater Goode 67
Fields, Terri. After the Death of Anna Gonzales 40
Fienberg, Anna. Borrowed Light 69
"Fine and Dandy" (Hawes) in Love & Sex:
    Ten Stories of Truth (Cart) 69
Fine, Anna. Flour Babies 68
Flaming, Allen, and Kate Scowen. My Crazy Life:
    How I Survived My Family 13
Fleischman, Paul. Whirligig 82
Flinn, Alex
    Breaking Point 90
    Breathing Underwater 77

Flour Babies (Fine) 68
Following My Own Footsteps (Hahn) 89
Foster's War (Reeder) 23
Frank, Lucy. I Am an Artichoke 48
Friendship 38, 86

G

Gallo, Paul. On the Fringe 91
Gamma Hydoxybutrate
    See Date rape drugs
Gardner, Howard 4
Gateway (Robinson) 61
"Geeks Bearing gifts" (Koertge) in
    On the Fringe (Gallo) 91
GHB
    See Date rape drugs
Giles, Gail. Shattering Glass 25
Gingerbread (Cohn) 62
Girls, The (Koss) 89
Give a Boy a Gun (Strasser) 92
Glovach, Linda. Beauty Queen 34
Go Ask Alice (Anonymous) 33
God of Beer (Keizer) 34, 82
Goobie, Beth. The Dream Where the Losers Go 55
Gossip Girl (Von Ziegesar) 92
Gottlieb, Lori. Stick Figure 48
Grant, Cynthia D. The White Horse 34
Greater Goode, A (Ferris), ... 67
Great Eye, The (Shalant) 61
Great Turkey Walk, The (Karr) 12
"Guns for Geeks" (Crutcher) in
    On the Fringe (Gallo) 91
Guy Time (Weeks) 62

H

Haddix, Margaret Peterson. Don't You Dare
    Read This, Mrs. Dunphrey 26
Hahn, Mary Downing. Following My Own Footsteps ... 89
Hanauer, Cathi. My Sister's Bones 49
Hanging on to Max (Bechard) 68
Hank's Story (Buchanan) 22
Hautzig, Deborah. Second Star to the Right 49
Hawes, Louise. "Fine and Dandy" in Love & Sex:
    Ten Stories of Truth (Bauer) 69
Heart of the City, The (Koertge) 33
Hero (Rottman) 27
Hersch, Patricia. A Tribe Apart: A Journey into
    the Heart of American Adolescence 122
Hiaasen, Carl. Hoot 89
High, Linda Oatman. The Summer of the
    Great Divide 60
Hobbs, Valerie. Charlie's Run 60
Hoot (Hiaasen) 89
Hornbacher, Marya. Wasted: A Memoir of Anorexia
    and Bulimia 50
Hrdlitschka, Shelley. Dancing Naked 69

I

I Am an Artichoke (Frank) 48
I Hadn't Meant to Tell You This (Woodson). 24
I Know What You Did Last Summer (Duncan). 81
Imani All Mine (Porter) 70
Interactive booktalking
    Driver's Ed (Cooney) 124
    steps in 104–105
    types of questions 105, 124
Internal assets
    See Resiliency
Internal locus of control. 8
Irwin, Cait. *Conquering the Beast Within:
    How I Fought Depression and Won…
    And How You Can, Too* 41
It Happened to Nancy (Sparks) 76
Izzy Will-Nilly (Voigt). 82

J

Jay's Journal (Sparks) 43
Jinx (Wild). 43
Junk (Burgess) 33

K

Karr, Kathleen. *The Great Turkey Walk*. 12
Kauai Longitudinal Study 8
Keeping the Moon (Dessen) 13
Keizer, Garret. *God of Beer* 34, 82
Kettlewell, Caroline. *Skin Game: A Memoir* 55
*Kim: Empty Inside: The Diary of An Anonymous
    Teenager* (Sparks). 50
Klass, David. *You Don't Know Me* 23
Koertge, Ron
    "Geeks Bearing Gifts" in *On the Fringe* (Gallo). . . 91
    Heart of the City, The 33
Koja, Kathe. *Straydog* 91
Konigsburg, e.l. *Silent to the Bone* 23
Koss, Amy Goldman
    Girls, The 89
    Stranger in Dadland 60
Koss, Mary P. 74

L

Leslie's Journal (Stratton) 78
Levenkron, Steven. *The Luckiest Girl in the World* 54
Levine, Gail Carson. "Pluto" in *On the Edge:
    Stories at the Brink* (Duncan) 26
Librarians and media specialists. 9–11
    hobbies. 11
    mentoring. 9–10
    resiliency 11
    social skills. 11
    teen programming 10
Library and school media programs
    teen-friendly environments 11
Life in the Fat Lane (Burnett). 49
Like Sisters on the Homefront (Williams-Garcia) 70
Losing Louisa (Caseley). 62

Love and Other Four-Letter Words (Mackler). 63
Love & Sex: Ten Stories of Truth (Cart) 69
Luckiest Girl in the World, The (Levenkron) 54
Lucy the Giant (Smith). 27

M

Mack, Tracy. *Drawing Lessons*. 61
Mackler, Carolyn. *Love and Other Four-Letter Words*. . . 63
Make Lemonade (Wolff). 71
Maltreatment 17–22
    causes of 18
    effect on brain 18
    extent of problem 18–19
    teens as victims 17
    vulnerability to problems 18
    See also Abuse
    See also Neglect
Maya's Divided World (Velásquez) 64
Mazer, Norma Fox. *When She Was Good* 26
McCormick, Patricia. *Cut*. 55
McNicoll, Sylvia. *Walking a Thin Line*. 50
Mental Health Warning Signs and Symptoms. . . viii, 15–16
Mickle, Shelley Fraser. *The Turning Hour* 42
Miklowitz, Gloria D. *Past Forgiving*. 77
Miller, Mary Beth. *Aimee*. 42
Ms. Magazine study of relationship violence 74
Multiple intelligences. 4–5
*My Crazy Life: How I Survived My
    Family* (Flaming and Scowen) 13
My Life in Dog Years (Paulsen). 12
My Sister's Bones (Hanauer) 49

N

National Highway Traffic Safety
    Administration 79
National League of Cities. 17
Neglect. 17–20
    characteristics of victims. 17–18
    educational. 19
    emotional 19
    physical 19
Newman, Lesléa. *Fat Chance*. 48
Nobody Else Has to Know (Tomey) 81
Night I Disappeared, The (Deaver). 25
Nolan, Han. *Born Blue*. 26

O

On the Edge: Stories at the Brink (Duncan) 26, 56
On the Fringe (Gallo). 91
Orr, Wendy. *Peeling the Onion* 82
Oughton, Jerrie. *Perfect Family* 68

P

Past Forgiving (Miklowitz) 77
Paulsen, Gary. *My Life in Dog Years*. 12
Peck, Richard. *Strays Like Us*. 33
Peeling the Onion (Orr) 82
Pennebaker, Ruth. *Don't Think Twice* 70

Index 131

Perfect Family (Oughton) 68
Physical abuse
    See Abuse, physical
Physical neglect
    See Neglect, physical
Plum-Ucci, Carol. *The Body of Christopher Creed* 91
Plummer, Louise. *A Dance for Three* 70
"Pluto" (Levine) in *On the Edge: Stories at
    the Brink* (Duncan) 26
Pollack, William S. *Real Boys' Voices* 87, 123
Ponton, Lynn E.
    *The Romance of Risk: Why Teenagers
        Do the Things They Do* 123
    *The Sex Lives of Teenagers: Revealing the
        Secret World of Adolescent Boys and Girls* . . 123
Porter, Connie. *Imani All Mine* 70
Powell, Randy. *Three Clams and an Oyster* 42
Pregnancy 65–67
    birth control 67
    characteristics of teen mothers 66
    comparison of pregnant teens to teens on
        birth control 66
    decreases in 65
    effective prevention programs 67
    frequency of teen sex 67
    girls most likely to become 66–67
    impact on children born to teen mothers 66
Pregnancy rates 65
Princess Diana 52
Problem-solving skills 5, 7, 10

Q
Quarles, Heather. *A Door Near Here* 27

R
Racing the Past (Deans) 88
Rats Saw God (Thomas) 34
Reading 3, 8, 124
    establishing lifelong habit 11
    promote resiliency 10
    to solve problems 10–11
Real Boys' Voices (Pollack) 87, 123
Reeder, Carolyn. *Foster's War* 23
Relationship violence 73–76
    acquaintance rape 75
    characteristics of perpetrator 73–74
Resiliency 7–11, 66, 86
    achievement-oriented activities 11
    characteristics of children and teens 7–8
    characteristics of adults 8
    competence skills 7
    depression 59
    definition (Benard) 7
    external assets 7, 9
    importance of book collections 9–10
    inability to overcome multiple challenges 8
    internal assets 8
    Kauai Longitudinal Study 8
    promote by connecting with teens 9

reactive problem focus model 8
    recommendations to librarians 9–11
    role model 103
    self-esteem 29, 59
Resiliency, importance of
    book collections 10
    career goals 8
    college 8
    hobbies 11
    reading 10
    social skills 9, 11
    teachers 9
Resiliency theory 9
Rivers, Karen. *Surviving Sam* 42
Robinson, Lee. *Gateway* 61
Rodowsky, Colby. *Spindrift* 61
*The Romance of Risk: Why Teenagers Do the
    Things They Do* (Ponton) 123
Roofies
    See Date rape drugs
Rope Burn (Siebold) 62
Roseanne 52
Rottman, S.L. *Hero* 27

S
Saint Jude (Wilson) 55
Say Yes (Couloumbis) 11
Scarred Soul, The (Alderman) 52, 53
Second Star to the Right (Hautzig) 49
Self-esteem
    See Resiliency
Self-inflicted violence 51–54
    characteristics of 51
    cutting 52–53
    effectiveness of 51, 53
    purpose of 51
    responding to 54
    ritualistic patterns of cutting 53
    three types of 52
    treatment 54
Self-injury
    See Self-inflicted violence
Serotonin 38, 46
*The Sex Lives of Teenagers: Revealing the Secret
    World of Adolescent Boys and Girls* (Ponton) 123
Sexual abuse
    See Abuse, sexual
Shalant, Phyllis. *The Great Eye* 61
Shattering Glass (Giles) 25
Shaw, Susan. *Black-eyed Suzie* 24
Siebold, Jan. *Rope Burn* 62
Silent to the Bone (Konigsburg) 23
Singer, Nicky. *Feather Boy* 90
Sister Split (Warner) 62
Skin Game: A Memoir (Kettlewell) 55
Smack (Burgess) 33
Smith, Sherri L. *Lucy the Giant* 28
Social skills 11
Someone Like You (Dessen) 69

Sparks, Beatrice
- *It Happened to Nancy* 76
- *Jay's Journal* 43
- *Kim: Empty Inside: The Diary of an Anonymous Teenager* 50
- *Treacherous Love: The Diary of an Anonymous Teenager* 27

Speak (Anderson) 76
Spindrift (Rodowsky) 61
Spinelli, Jerry. *Stargirl* 13
Stargirl (Spinelli) 13
Staying Fat for Sarah Byrnes (Crutcher) 25
"Stevie in the Mirror" (Wittlinger) in *On the Edge: Stories at the Brink* (Duncan) ... 56
Stick Figure (Gottlieb) 48
Stranger in Dadland (Koss) 60
Strasser, Todd. *Give a Boy a Gun* 92
Stratton, Allan. *Leslie's Journal* 78
Straydog (Koja) 91
Strays Like Us (Peck) 33
Substance use and abuse 29–32, 52
- alcohol 30
- among youth 30, 75
- at-risk factors 29, 52, 66
- behaviors indicating use 31
- depression 31
- marijuana 30–31
- popularity of drugs 30
- prevention programs 29, 31–32
- tobacco 29, 30

Suicide 39–40, 51
- means invoked by boys 39
- means invoked by girls 39
- pattern of 39
- prevention 40
- previous attempts 39

Suicide ideation 39
Summer of the Great Divide, The (High) 60
Surviving Sam (Rivers) 42

T

Tangerine (Bloor) 88
Teachers, resiliency 9
Teen pregnancy
  See Pregnancy
Tears of a Tiger (Draper) 41, 81
Technology 4–5, 104
Ten Miles from Winnemucca (Wyss) 64
That Summer (Dessen) 63
Third National Incidence Study of Child Abuse and Neglect 18–19
This Lullaby (Dessen) 63
Thomas, Rob. *Rats Saw God* 34
Three Clams and an Oyster (Powell) 42
Tomey, Ingrid. *Nobody Else Has to Know* 81
Top-Secret Journal of Fiona Clair Jardin, The (Cruise) 60

Treacherous Love: The Diary of an Anonymous Teenager (Sparks) 27
Tribe Apart: A Journey into the Heart of American Adolescence, A (Hersch) 122
True Believer (Wolff) 71
True Colors of Caitlynne Jackson, The (Williams) 24
Tune In Anytime (Cooney) 63
Turning Hour, The (Mickle) 42

U

U.S. Advisory Board on Child Abuse and Neglect 17

V

Velásquez, Gloria. *Maya's Divided World* 64
Voigt, Cynthia
- *Izzy Willy-Nilly* 82
- *When She Hollers* 28

Von Ziegesar, Cecily. *Gossip Girl* 92

W

Walking a Thin Line (McNicoll) 50
Warner, Sally. *Sister Split* 62
Wasted: A Memoir of Anorexia and Bulimia (Hornbacher) 50
Weeks, Sarah. *Guy Time* 62
Werner, Emmy E. and Ruth S. Smith 8
  See also Kauai Longitudinal Study
  See also Resiliency
Whale Talk (Crutcher) 90
What Happened on Planet Kid (Conly) 23
When She Hollers (Voigt) 28
When She Was Good (Mazer) 26
Whirligig (Fleischman) 82
White Horse, The (Grant) 34
Wild, Margaret. *Jinx* 43
Williams, Carol Lynch. *The True Colors of Caitlynne Jackson* 24
Williams-Garcia, Rita. *Like Sisters on the Homefront* 70
Wilson, Dawn. *Saint Jude* 55
Wittlinger, Ellen. "Stevie in the Mirror" in *On the Edge: Stories at the Brink* (Duncan) 56
Wolff, Virginia Euwer
- *Make Lemonade* 71
- *True Believer* 71

Woodson, Jacqueline. *I Hadn't Meant to Tell You This* 24
Wyss, Thelma Hatch. *Ten Miles from Winnemucca* 64

Y

You Don't Know Me (Klass) 23
You Remind Me of You: A Poetry Memoir (Corrigan) ... 49

About the Author

Jami Biles Jones is a media specialist at Barron Collier High School in Naples, Florida, and teaches online courses in educational media for Nova Southeastern University in Ft. Lauderdale, Florida. In addition to school library media experience, the author has directed public libraries in New Jersey and North Carolina and worked in state libraries in Delaware and Arizona. In 2002, Dr. Jones became a member of the first cohort of media specialists to achieve National Board Certification. Dr. Jones is the creator of the Florida Association of Media in Education's Amanda Award that recognizes media specilaists who develop programs that promote teen resiliency and self-esteem.

Dr Jones received a BA in Sociology from Mills College, an MLS from the University of Maryland, and a Ph.D. in Information Sciences from Nova Southeastern University. The author can be contacted through her Web site at <http://www.askdrjami.org>.

www.ingramcontent.com/pod-product-compliance
Lightning Source LLC
Chambersburg PA
CBHW080412300426
44113CB00015B/2494